Mary Magdalene

A Personal Connection

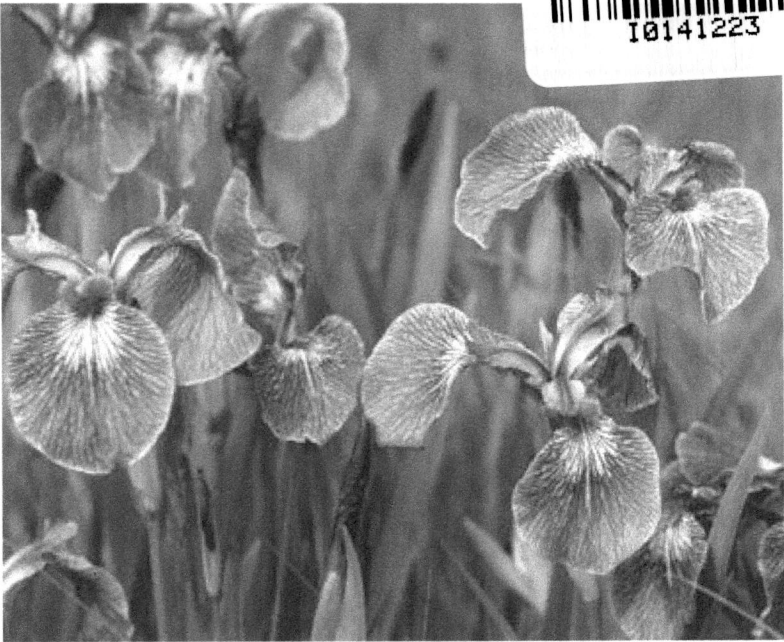

Michele Doucette, M. Ed.

Mary Magdalene: A Personal Connection

ISBN 978-1-935786-78-8

Printed in the United States of America by

St. Clair Publications

PO Box 726

McMinnville, TN   37111-0726

stclairpublications.com

Table of Contents

Preface

Considered a prostitute, by the Roman Catholic Church for the past 2000 years, it may never be possible to determine the real role of Mary Magdalene, given that her influence has been deliberately obscured by the ravages of time. Interestingly enough, neither the Eastern Orthodox tradition nor the Gnostic tradition have ever portrayed her in such a manner.

The Eastern Church has always honored her as an apostle, noting her as *the apostle to the apostles*, based on the account of the <u>Gospel of John</u> which has Jesus calling her by name and telling her to give the news of his resurrection to the other disciples.

Upon deliverance of Homily 33 in 591 AD, it was Pope Gregory who asserted that Mary Magdalene, Mary (sister of Martha and Lazarus of Bethany) and the unnamed sinner in Luke (the one who anoints Christ's feet) were one and the same; hence, the repentant sinner, the woman caught in adultery, had become the prostitute, the whore, the harlot.

1

While the RCC officially reversed this conflation in 1969, the power of "one pope to change the world's perception of a Biblical character, hundreds of years after the fact, and for over a thousand years into the future" [1] should give one considerable pause for thought.

No formal apology was ever put forth; the reversal simply stated that the 6th century rationale for determining that the three women were one and the same had no sound scriptural, or logical, basis.

In essence, the RCC was not saying *we mistakenly identified Mary Magdalene as a whore*; instead, the reversal simply implied that *we mistakenly identified Mary Magdalene with the 'fallen woman' in Luke's gospel, and with Mary of Bethany.*

Revealed in September 2012, there is a business-card size fragment of 4th century papyrus (written in Coptic, an ancient Egyptian language) that appears to suggest that some

---

[1] https://www.theosophical.org/publications/1531

people, in ancient times, believed that Jesus and Mary Magdalene were married. [2] [3] [4]

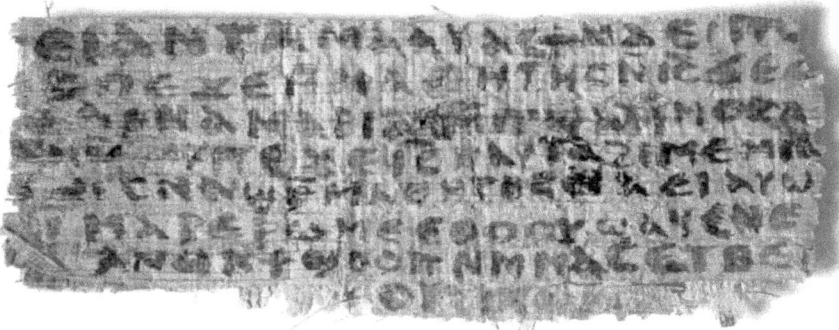

Karen L. King (Harvard Divinity School Professor)

---

[2] https://www.nytimes.com/2012/09/19/us/historian-says-piece-of-papyrus-refers-to-jesus-wife.html
[3] https://www.livescience.com/34229-what-does-the-gospel-of-jesus-s-wife-say.html
[4] https://www.livescience.com/23284-jesus-wife-gospel-suggests.html

1 ｜ⲛⲁ]ⲉⲓ ⲁⲛ ⲧⲁⲙⲁⲁⲩ ⲁⲥⲧ ⲛⲁⲉⲓ ⲡⲱ[ⲛϩ   1] "not [to] me. My mother gave to me li[fe..."

2 ｜ⲥ ⲡⲉⲝⲉ ⲛ̄ⲙⲁⲑⲏⲧⲏⲥ ⲓ̄ⲥ̄ ⲝⲉ ⲥ[2] The disciples said to Jesus, ".[

3 ｜]. ⲁⲣⲛⲁ ⲙⲁⲣⲓⲁⲙ ⲙ̄ⲡ̄ϣⲁ ⲙ̄ⲙⲟⲥ ⲁ[ⲛ(?)   3] deny. Mary is worthy of it[35] [

4 ｜]...../ ⲡⲉⲝⲉ ⲓ̄ⲥ̄ ⲛⲁⲩ ⲧⲁϩⲓⲙⲉ ⲙ̄ⲛ̄[4]......" Jesus said to them, "My wife ..[

5 ｜]...ⲥ ⲛⲁϣⲣⲙⲁⲑⲏⲧⲏⲥ ⲛⲁⲉⲓ ⲁⲩⲱ [5]... she will be able to be my disciple .. [

6 ｜] ⲓ ⲙⲁⲣⲉⲣⲱⲙⲉ ⲉⲑⲟⲟⲩ ϣⲁϥⲉ ⲛⲉ[6] Let wicked people swell up ... [

7 ｜]. ⲁⲛⲟⲕ ϯϣⲟⲟⲡ ⲛⲙⲙⲁⲥ ⲉⲧⲃⲉ ⲡ[7] As for me, I dwell with her in order to . [

8 papyrus broken off ±6] . ⲟⲩϩⲓⲕⲱⲛ ..[8] an image [

9 (illegible traces of ink)

---

[35] Or alternatively: Mary is n[ot] worthy of it.

Karen L. King (Harvard Divinity School Professor)

Copyright © 2012

4

Whilst part of the text identified reads ... *Jesus said to them, My wife* ... it is important to state that the name of this wife is not given.

Immediately below the line about Jesus having a wife, the papyrus includes a second provocative clause that purportedly says, *she will be able to be my disciple.*

In conjunction with the fact that Mary Magdalene was the first to be charged with the supreme ministry of proclaiming the Christian message, it seems credible that she was both wife and disciple of Jesus.

The synoptic Gospels give us very little information with regards to Mary Magdalene, but according to Jean-Yves Leloup, author of The Gospel of Mary Magdalene (published in 2002 by Inner Traditions International), they all agree on four central points; namely, [1] she was one of Christ's female followers, [2] she was present at the crucifixion, [3] she was the sole witness of his resurrection and [4] she was the first to be charged with the supreme ministry of proclaiming the Christian message.

Disillusioned

My parents were legally (and officially) divorced when I was 15 years old; of course, this came after a lengthy period whereby the marriage had first to be annulled (or dissolved).

It is one thing to dissolve a marital union, but quite another to dissolve physical bodies. Does this, then, mean that my sisters and I had been demoted? In truth, this political move was reminiscent of firstly being declared one's legal heir before being relegated to that of bastard.

By this time, it was becoming more and more difficult, for me, to continue to maintain my staunch belief in a religious institution that would utilize such a procedure to declare a marriage null and void, merely as a means to maintain, or hold onto, current flock in the hopes of perpetuating, and adding to, the overall body; a whimsical farce, to put it mildly.

Not only did I believe that Jesus could well have been married, and had a family, so, too, did I believe that the church had no right to disempower their priests by insisting upon a vow of chastity (associated with the supposed mindset that it would bring one closer to God).

In the knowingness that there just had to be something more, my search had begun.

Some would even venture to say that I had embarked on the road to eternal hell and damnation.

Always Questions

As long as I can remember, there have been countless questions reverberating inside my head. As I began to delve further into my own research, these unanswered questions seemed to increase at an exponential rate.

Who was Mary Magdalene?

Was she the repentant sinner, the notorious adulteress, the prostitute, the whore, the harlot?

Was she a priestess from a royal family?

Was she the trusted apostle of Jesus?

Was she the Gnostic Sophia?

Was she the wife of the man we have come to know as Jesus?

What is it that Mary Magdalene represents?

Why does an existential tension exist between male and female?

The chapters that follow delineate my research, my queries, my thoughts, my comments, my reflections, my ponderings.

Prehistoric Times

Prior to the patriarchy that exists today, it has been written that ours was a matrifocal culture wherein women were the primary life-givers and nurturers; hence, there existed a much stronger connection to Mother Earth.

In keeping, these matrifocal societies were very egalitarian whereby both sexes were honored, revered and respected; so, too, were these societies non-violent, non-warring and very creative. [5]

Mother Earth is the life force that connects all as one.

At this time, she was honored as the living organism that she is; nature was respected, not dominated, decimated and destroyed. [6]

---

[5] Briar, Kathy. *In Search of The Feminine Divine*. Retrieved March 8, 2007 from www.gaiafriends.org/search.txt.html
[6] Ibid.

Merlin Stone, author of <u>When God was a Woman</u>, states that "the Upper Paleolithic period, though most of its sites have been found in Europe, is the *conjectural* foundation of the religion of the Goddess as it emerged in the Near East." [7]

As fascinated as I am by the all powerful, all loving, splendid and benevolent Mother, I am not here to debate the issue, one way or another, for this is not my area of study.

My belief in the Goddess is not one that is based on archaeological evidence, conjecture or politics; my belief is naught but an inner spiritual one.

In truth, we do not know what happened between men and women in prehistoric times; neither can we determine whether or not patriarchy was a human universal or a more recent historical phenomenon. [8]

---

[7] Stone, Merlin. (1978) <u>When God Was A Woman</u> (page 10).New York, New York: Mariner Books.
[8] https://www.nytimes.com/books/first/e/eller-myth.html

Ingenious Idea

A polytheistic religion that involved the worship of many gods, the Romans believed their success, as a world power, could only be attributed to maintaining collective good relations with the gods.

While the Hebrews could be excused for their refusal to follow this religion, by virtue of the undoubted fact that their monotheism was an ancient national tradition, it was the Christians who were fast becoming a threat to the overall cohesiveness of Roman society. [9]

Eventually, the profession of Christianity was defined as a capital crime; one could only gain pardon by apostasy, (rejection of a faith once confessed) as demonstrated by

---

[9]

http://realhistoryww.com/world_history/ancient/Misc/Christianity2.htm

making a sacrifice to either the pagan gods or the Emperor.
[10]

In February 303 AD, the worst of all persecutions erupted under the co-emperors Diocletian and Galerius; Christians were arrested, tortured, mutilated, burned, starved, and condemned to gladiatorial contests to amuse spectators. [11]

In April 311 AD, Galerius, senior emperor of the Tetrarchy, issued an edict of toleration; although property was not restored, Christians were finally granted the right to practice their religion. [12] [13]

---

[10]

http://realhistoryww.com/world_history/ancient/Misc/Christianity2.htm

[11]

https://en.wikipedia.org/wiki/Constantine_the_Great_and_Christianity

[12]

https://en.wikipedia.org/wiki/Edict_of_Toleration_by_Galerius

[13] https://sourcebooks.fordham.edu/source/edict-milan.asp

What needs to be understood is that Christianity did not begin as a religion; instead, it was *the movement of a group of people around a single charismatic teacher or preacher.*

Two years later, in February 313 AD, Christianity was officially legalized by Emperor Constantine in his Edict of Milan. [14] Adopting Christianity as his system of belief after the Battle of Milvian Bridge [15] in 312 AD, Constantine had problems with his new faith. Based on tenets that condemned worldly authority while also insisting on a life that was non-worldly, individualistic and non-political, Constantine stated that the foundational Christian texts were not only anti-Roman (for Judea was part of the Roman Empire during the life of Jesus of Nazareth), but so, too, were they dismissive of human worldly authority. [16]

---

[14] https://en.wikipedia.org/wiki/Edict_of_Milan
[15] https://en.wikipedia.org/wiki/Battle_of_Milvian_Bridge
[16]
http://realhistoryww.com/world_history/ancient/Misc/Christianity2.htm

If Christianity was going to work as a religion in a state ruled by a monarch who considered himself divine, whilst also demanding worship and absolute authority, there were going to have to be some major changes, given that ......

→there were as many forms of Christianity as there were communities of Christians

→there was no established or unifying doctrine

→the church was severely divided over fundamental questions

Needing a unified church, it was the schism between the Arians and the Athanasians that propelled Constantine into action.

The Arian concept of Christ was that the Son of God did not always exist, but was created by God the Father, meaning that God the Father was not the same as God the Son; hence, Jesus *could not be* divine.

The Athanasian concept of Christ was that Christ the Son is of the same substance as God the Father; hence, Jesus *was* divine.

If the church was going to be one of consolidation for its people, these two separate approaches had to be unified. Ossius (or Hosius) of Cordova, Constantine's trusted spiritual advisor, had failed in his mission to bring about the much needed reconciliation.

In summoning the First Ecumenical Council of the church, [17] the opening session was held on 20 May 325 AD, in the great hall of the palace at Nicaea, with Constantine himself presiding and giving the opening speech. [18]

The teachings of Arius were condemned; as a result, he was excommunicated in 318 AD.

---

[17]

http://realhistoryww.com/world_history/ancient/Misc/Christianity2.htm

[18] Ibid.

The council formulated a creed that became known as the Nicene Creed; a creed [19] that affirms the nature of the three persons comprising the Trinity (God the Father, God the Son, God the Holy Spirit), thereby confirming the doctrine of consubstantiality (of one and the same substance) as adhered to by Athanasius of Alexandria. [20]

In 331 AD, Constantine ordered that an ecumenical Bible be written; a Bible that would be acceptable to pagans as well as Christians, and Eusebius, the Bishop of Caesaria, a follower of Origen, [21] was assigned the task.

Dr. Gregory, a recent scholar in the field of manuscripts, believes that the Vatican [22] and Sinai [23] manuscripts are two of Constantine's fifty bibles. It is also important to share, herein, that the early Christians rejected these manuscripts.

---

[19] https://en.wikipedia.org/wiki/Nicene_creed
[20] https://en.wikipedia.org/wiki/Athanasius_of_Alexandria
[21] www.1611kingjamesbible.com/origen.html/
[22] www.1611kingjamesbible.com/codex_vaticanus.html/
[23] www.1611kingjamesbible.com/codex_sinaiticus.html/

Constantine's legitimized version of Christianity allowed for human authority and power as opposed to the anti-political ideas of Jesus of Nazareth; a version of Christianity that has existed to this day.

At best, it may have been a blend of paganism and Christianity, purely for political purposes.

My personal conjecture is that this religion, foisted upon the populace, albeit a most lucrative plan, was created to completely control and dominate, not only human beings, but what they thought, what they believed and what they perceived.

Lucrative Plan

The Vicar of Christ, or *Vicarius Christi*, is a term, in keeping with the Papacy, that generally refers to the earthly representative of God or Christ; a most specific term, first appearing in the 5th century, it was used in reference to the Bishop of Rome (also known as the Pope). [24]

Interestingly, *Vicarius Filii Dei*, meaning Vicar of the Son of God, as in a physical representative, is a phrase that was first used in the medieval Donation of Constantine to refer to Saint Peter, a leader of the Early Christian Church who is regarded as the first Pope by the Catholic Church. [25] [26] [27]

In truth, this forged document was an imperial decree by which the Byzantine Emperor Constantine supposedly transferred authority, over Rome and the western part of the Roman Empire, to the Pope.

---

[24] https://en.wikipedia.org/wiki/Vicar_of_Christ
[25] https://en.wikipedia.org/wiki/Vicarius_Filii_Dei
[26] https://en.wikipedia.org/wiki/Donation_of_Constantine
[27] https://en.wikipedia.org/wiki/Constantine_I

Constantine founded the City of Constantinople in 324 AD and yet the document *was said to have been signed* in 315 AD.

Fraudulently proclaimed to be the Vicar of Christ, this concocted document set forth a new precedent: the local bishop of Rome (aka the Pope) *could now sanction who became king.*

In 496 AD, the Roman Church was not the dominant establishment, meaning that it was in competition with other groups (such as Arianism, for example).

Following his own conversion, tt was King Clovis I who was responsible for persuading much of Western Europe to convert to Christianity, thereby "firmly establishing Catholicism as the dominant religion within the Merovingian Kingdom, and saving the Church from almost certain collapse." [28]

---

[28] https://www.juneaustin.co.uk/mysteries/merovingians

The Church "agreed to pledge their allegiance to Clovis and promised that a new Holy Empire would be established under the auspices of the Merovingians." [29]

Having been proclaimed *Novus Constantinus* (emperor of a to-be-created Holy Roman Empire; a title which translates to the *New Constantine*), Clovis agreed to use his armies to crush any denominations that were in direct competition with the Roman church.

When they granted him this title, Clovis had no reason to doubt the sincerity of the Church, but "unbeknownst to him, he had unwittingly become a pawn in a conspiracy for the Church to eventually seize control of his Kingdom, thereby establishing the Pope as the supreme ruler." [30]

———————————◆———————————

Let us now fast forward to Dagobert II (son of Sigebert, grandson of Lothar and great grandson of Clovis I, also of the Merovingian line).

---

[29] https://www.juneaustin.co.uk/mysteries/merovingians
[30] Ibid.

Born in 651 AD, it is said that because he was lax in serving the wishes of the Roman church, thereby incurring "ecclesiastical displeasure," he was assassinated on December 23, 679 AD. [31] [32]

The successive Mayors of the Palace ......

[1] Pépin II (circa 635 to 714; the first Duke of the Franks and father of Charles Martel, illegitimate son through his mistress, Alpaida),

[2] Charles Martel (circa 686 to 741; grandfather of Charlemagne) and

[3] Pépin III, also called Pépin the Short (circa 714 to 768; father of Charlemagne)

...... continued to gain in personal power.

Pépin III, however, was not satisfied with being Mayor; he wanted to be king.

---

[31] doubleuoglobe.com/vol11/cn11-79.html

[32] https://www.juneaustin.co.uk/mysteries/merovingians

Coming to an arrangement with the Pope, by virtue of a spuriously forged document, none other than the <u>Donation of Constantine</u> (mysteriously discovered in 751 AD and supposedly written some 400 years earlier), he was proclaimed king, leading to the removal, and imprisonment, of the true Merovingian king, Childeric III. [33] [34] [35] [36] [37]

As a means of further legitimizing his claim, as is generally the case with royalty, he married Bertrada of Laon, daughter of Charibert of Laon and great granddaughter of Bertrada of Prüm, a Merovingian princess.

The power now belonged to Rome.

[33] https://en.wikipedia.org/wiki/Pepin_II_the_Middle
[34] https://en.wikipedia.org/wiki/Charles_Martel
[35] https://en.wikipedia.org/wiki/Pepin_the_Short
[36] doubleuoglobe.com/vol11/cn11-79.html
[37] https://en.wikipedia.org/wiki/Childeric_III

Desposyni

Following the fall of Jerusalem in 70 CE (some 40 years after the crucifixion), an Imperial decree issued by Emperor Vesparion ordered "the family of David to be sought, that no one might be left among the Jews who was of the royal stock." [38] Although many were seized, some were released and it was upon their release that they became "leaders of the churches in a strict dynastic progression, because they had borne testimony and because they were of the Lord's family." [39]

These persecuted descendants were called the *Desposyni*, meaning heirs of the Lord.

---

[38] Crusé, Christian Frederick, translator. (1856) <u>The Ecclesiastical History of Eusebius Pamphilus, Bishop of Cesarea, in Palestine</u>. New York, NY: Thomas N. Stanford. Book 3, Chapter XII, page 99. Can be viewed online at https://archive.org/details/ecclesiasticalhi00euse

[39] https://www.esolibris.com/articles/alternative_history/magdalene-legacy.php

The Vatican Archive reveals that, in 318 CE, a delegation of Messianic descendants confronted Sylvester, the Bishop of Rome (the Pope). They were insistent in their beliefs, stating that the Nazarene Church of Jesus was being corrupted, and that it should rightly be led by the family heirs, not by a despotic Imperial regime. [40] They were quickly advised that the power of salvation did not rest with Jesus, but with Emperor Constantine, for whom the right of Messianic inheritance had been personally "reserved since the beginning of time." [41]

Interestingly, the key monarchies of Europe were of Davidic descent; some in the direct lineage of the *Desposyni* heirs of Jesus.

In effect, all efforts to demolish these successions had failed.

---

[40] https://www.pressreader.com/ireland/sunday-independent-ireland/20070304/282222301297251
[41]

https://www.esolibris.com/articles/alternative_history/magdalene-legacy.php

The only way that the Papal Court could establish its supreme position was to take control of the monarchical structure; in 751, Pope Zachary managed to contrive a way to achieve these means. [42] Without revealing his source, Zachary was able to produce a hitherto previously unknown document, that was seemingly 400 years old; one that carried the signature of Emperor Constantine.

Proclaiming the Pope to be Christ's personally elected representative on Earth, this document stated that only he had the power and authority to *create* kings and queens as his subordinates. [43]

By virtue of this document, the Donation of Constantine, the whole nature and structure of monarchy changed from being an office of community guardianship to one of absolute rule; henceforth, European monarchs were crowned by the Pope, becoming servants of the Church instead of being servants to

---

42

https://www.esolibris.com/articles/alternative_history/magd alene-legacy.php

[43] Ibid.

the people. [44] The expired Roman Empire suddenly blossomed into a new concept: a Holy Roman Empire controlled from the Vatican. [45]

Pope Zachary's first initiative was to depose the most influential of all royal houses: the Merovingian Kings of Gaul (France); boasting a genealogical descent from King David of Israel, this enigmatic dynasty had been Lords of the Franks for 300 years. [46] In keeping with the 1st-century edict of Emperor Vespasian, one that ordered *the family of David to be sought, that no one might be left among the Jews who was of the royal stock*, the Merovingian line should never have existed, as far as Zachary was concerned; he had King Childeric III seized and incarcerated. [47]

In his place, Zachary installed a family of hitherto regional Mayors of the Palace, subsequently styled Carolingians.

44

https://www.esolibris.com/articles/alternative_history/magdalene-legacy.php
[45] Ibid.
[46] Ibid.
[47] Ibid.

Throughout the 236 years of Carolingian monarchy, the only king of any significance was the legendary Charlemagne; nevertheless, a new tradition had been born, with the Holy Roman Empire having become the new reality.

Kilmore Church

Kilmore Church (located in Dervaig)

Copyright © Barry Dunford

There is a striking stained glass window (a portion of the picture that graces the cover of this book) that can be located in a church, on the Scottish western Isle of Mull, that was built in 1905.

We know that Stephen Adam, a leading Scottish stained glass artist, produced this explosively symbolic piece, one year later, in 1906.

As per the cover of this book, the window shows a young man portrayed with the usual features attributed to Jesus (which also includes the traditional Nazarite central parting of the hair) with a halo above his head, holding hands with a woman without a halo. [48]

The woman is portrayed to be pregnant, her girdle painted below her abdomen rather than around her waist; the key to the identity of this woman is made plain by the text which appears immediately below the pregnant woman. [49]

Upon enlarging the text that accompanies the stained glass window, one is able to read ......

---

[48] Dunford, Barry. *Sacred Connections: Holy Land of Scotland and The Gospel of the Grail* website. Retrieved on March 8, 2007
sacredconnections.co.uk/index.php/stained-glass-window-mystery/
[49] Ibid.

Copyright © Barry Dunford

Barry Dunford goes further to say that this statement was made by none other than Jesus himself, and that it related directly to Mary Magdalene, sometimes referred to as Mary of Bethany, a statement that can be referenced in the Gospel of Luke (10: verse 42) with the complete and relevant text also located therein (10: verses 38-42).

———————✳———————

38: Now it came to pass, as they went, that he entered into a certain village: and a certain woman named Martha received him into her house.

39: And she had a sister called Mary, which also sat at Jesus' feet, and heard his word.

40: But Martha was cumbered about much serving, and came to him, and said, Lord, dost thou not care that my sister hath left me to serve alone? bid her therefore that she help me.

41: And Jesus answered and said unto her, Martha, Martha, thou art careful and troubled about many things:

42: But one thing is needful: and Mary hath chosen that good part, which shall not be taken away from her.

It certainly seems clear to Barry Dunford, as well as other Holy Bloodline believers, that the couple holding hands are, none other than, Jesus and Mary Magdalene, especially in reference to the Gospel text as cited above.

It is now queried as to who commissioned Stephen Adam to create this enigmatic and symbolic piece. In addition, what were the reasons for placing it in this particular church?

It has been claimed that a son of Jesus and Mary Magdalene was born on the holy Isle of Iona and, curiously, this stained glass window is to be found just eighteen miles away in Kilmore Church, Dervaig, on the Scottish Isle of Mull. Clearly, a mystery abounds.

My personal resonance with the belief that Jesus and Mary Magdalene may have been married, thereby creating a holy and sacred union, appeared to be my diving point into esoteric realms, previously unknown and unexplored.

If Jesus and Mary Magdalene were married and had children, why is it that the canonical Gospels make no mention of it? There is, in actual fact, very little in the Gospels that provides us with details during the time in which Jesus lived; hence, it becomes necessary to delve into other sources in an attempt to sort through what may be missing pieces of a most intriguing puzzle.

I am sure that the reader will find these BBS Radio Show Recordings to be of great interest.

[1] Jeshua [50]

[2] Jeshua and Mary Magdalene 1 [51]

[3] Jeshua and Mary Magdalene 2 [52]

[4] Jeshua (with a message from Mary Magdalene) [53]

[5] The Mystical Jeshua [54]

---

[50]

www.metatronminutes.net/BBS_Radio/The_Messenger_201
0-10-2%20-%20Jeshua.mp3

[51]

www.metatronminutes.net/BBS_Radio/The_Messenger_201
0-10-9%20-%20Jeshua%20&%20Mary%20Magdalene.mp3

[52]

www.metatronminutes.net/BBS_Radio/The_Messenger_201
0-10-16%20-
%20Jeshua%20&%20Mary%20Magdalene%202.mp3

[53]

www.metatronminutes.net/BBS_Radio/The_Messenger_201
1-05-14%20-%20Jeshua.mp3

[54]

www.metatronminutes.net/BBS_Radio/The_Messenger_201
1-12-31%20-%20The%20Mystical%20Jeshua.mp3

[6] Jeshua [55]

[7] Mary Magdalene [56]

---

[55]

www.metatronminutes.net/BBS_Radio/The_Messenger_201
2-01-14%20-%20Jeshua.mp3

[56]

www.metatronminutes.net/BBS_Radio/Mary_Magdalene.m
p3

A Most Intriguing Puzzle

While the New Testament contains no explicit answer to the question of Jesus' marital state, I am most intrigued by the business-card size fragment of 4th century papyrus, written in Coptic (an ancient Egyptian language), that appears to suggest that some people, in ancient times, believed that Jesus and Mary Magdalene were married. [57] [58] [59]

While the papyrus does not prove anything, just knowing that such an early Christian community *believed* that Jesus was married is significant; a belief that may have gone back to the historical Jesus, meaning that the second generation of Christians found the assertion entirely plausible.

---

[57] https://www.nytimes.com/2012/09/19/us/historian-says-piece-of-papyrus-refers-to-jesus-wife.html
[58] https://www.livescience.com/34229-what-does-the-gospel-of-jesus-s-wife-say.html
[59] https://www.livescience.com/23284-jesus-wife-gospel-suggests.html

A New Gospel Revealed [60] [61]

Did Jesus Have a Wife? [62]

Jesus Had a Wife, says Scientists, as Ancient Papyrus Scroll Verified [63]

Jesus, Mary Magdalene and the Truth [64]

Jesus married Mary Magdalene and had children, according to ancient manuscript at the British Library [65] [66]

---

[60] harvardmagazine.com/2012/09/new-gospel

[61] https://www.bethinking.org/Media/PDF/King_JesusSaidToThem_draft_0917.pdf

[62] prospect.org/article/did-jesus-have-wife

[63] https://www.independent.co.uk/news/world/americas/jesus-had-a-wife-say-scientists-as-ancient-papyrus-scroll-verified-9255110.html

[64] www.mastermason.com/hiramdiscovered/jesussecret.html

[65] www.dailymail.co.uk/news/article-2827310/Jesus-married-prostitute-Mary-Magdalene-two-children-lost-gospel-reveals.html

[66] https://www.ibtimes.com/lost-gospel-book-claims-jesus-christ-married-mary-magdalene-had-two-children-1721418

Mary Magdalene's Secret [67]

Rosa Templum: The Enigmatic Arcanum of Rosslyn Chapel and the Bride of Christ (Barry Dunford) [68]

Scholarly Smackdown: Were Mary Magdalene and Jesus Married? [69]

Tests Reveal *Gospel of Jesus' Wife* Not Fake [70]

Tests Suggest *Gospel of Jesus' Wife* Is Authentic [71]

The Inside Story of a Controversial New Text About Jesus [72]

---

[67] www.beliefnet.com/Entertainment/Movies/The-Da-Vinci-Code/Mary-Magdalenes-Secret.aspx

[68] http://www.electricscotland.com/bible/connections2.htm

[69] www.beliefnet.com/Entertainment/Movies/The-Da-Vinci-Code/Scholarly-Smackdown-Were-Mary-Magdalene-And-Jesus-Married.aspx

[70] https://www.history.com/news/tests-reveal-gospel-of-jesuss-wife-not-fake

[71] https://www.livescience.com/44748-gospel-of-jesus-wife-authentic.html

[72] https://www.smithsonianmag.com/history/the-inside-story-of-a-controversial-new-text-about-jesus-41078791/

The Magdalene Legacy: Revelations Beyond the Da Vinci Code [73]

The Marriage of Jesus (Dr. Barbara Thiering) [74]

The Marriage of Jesus and Mary Magdalene [75]

The True Jesus and Mary Magdalene [76]

Was Jesus Married? (an 11 part series) [77]

Were Mary Magdalene and Jesus Married? [78]

---

[73]

https://www.esolibris.com/articles/alternative_history/magdalene-legacy.php

[74]

www.peshertechnique.infinitesoulutions.com/index_Marriage_of_Jesus.html

[75]

www.mastermason.com/hiramdiscovered/Marriagejesus.html

[76] www.thetruejesus.org

[77]

https://thebiblicalapologist.wordpress.com/2012/05/24/was-jesus-married-part-1-a-wiki-answers-discussion/

[78] www.lightparty.com/Spirituality/JesusMaryMarried.html

Who Was Mary Magdalene? [79]

MARY MAGDALENE: HER STORY WILL BE TOLD [80]

[81]

https://www.eventfinda.co.nz/2018/mary-

magdalene/auckland/papakura

---

[79] https://www.smithsonianmag.com/history/who-was-mary-magdalene-119565482/

[80] http://www.patheos.com/blogs/filmchat/2017/11/watch-first-trailer-mary-magdalene-starring-rooney-mara-joaquin-phoenix.html

[81] http://www.patheos.com/blogs/filmchat/2018/02/watch-mary-magdalene-jesus-challenge-conventional-thinking-second-international-trailer-mary-magdalene.html

Holy Blood, Holy Grail

Michael Baigent, Richard Leigh, and Henry Lincoln developed, and popularized, the hypothesis that a bloodline from Jesus and Mary Magdalene eventually became the Merovingian dynasty in their book The Holy Blood and the Holy Grail, in which they asserted [82] ......

The symbolic significance of Jesus is that he is God exposed to the spectrum of human experience; exposed to the first-hand knowledge of what being a man entails.

But could God, incarnate as Jesus, truly claim to be a man, to encompass the spectrum of human experience, without coming to know two of the most basic, most elemental facets of the human condition?

---

[82] Baigent, Michael, Leigh, Richard and Lincoln, Henry. (1983) Holy Blood, Holy Grail: The Secret History of Jesus, the Shocking Legacy of the Grail (page 409). New York, New York: Delacorte Press.

Could God claim to know the totality of human existence without confronting two such essential aspects of humanity as sexuality and paternity?

We do not think so.

In fact, we do not think the Incarnation truly symbolizes what it is intended to symbolize unless Jesus were married and sired children.

The Jesus of the Gospels, and of established Christianity, is ultimately incomplete; a God whose incarnation as man is only partial.

The Jesus who emerged from our research enjoys, in our opinion, a much more valid claim to what Christianity would have him be.

———————————❖———————————

In keeping with their living and plausible Jesus, one shown to be both meaningful and comprehensible to readers of the 20th century, it is my personal belief that he was married and had a family.

Like the British Royal Family, so, too, am I able to trace my genealogy back to the early Middle Ages, the period of European history lasting from the 5th century to approximately 1000 AD.

The Merovingians established themselves in the former Roman provinces in Gaul, and Clovis I, following his victory over the Alemanni at the Battle of Tolbiac in 496 AD, converted to Catholicism, laying the foundation of the Frankish Empire, the dominant state of medieval Western Christendom.

Starting with the Frankish realms at the beginning of the 9th century, Charlemagne united much of modern day France, western Germany and northern Italy into the Carolingian Empire.

Scholarship and Classical learning flourished under Charlemagne leading to what 20th century historians called the Carolingian Renaissance.

At this time, however, there are no documented records to prove a lineage of four centuries from Jesus to the Merovingian kings.

Waiting to be rediscovered in the British Library is an ancient manuscript of the early Church, copied by an anonymous monk; the manuscript is at least 1450 years old, possibly dating to the first century (Jesus' lifetime).

The Lost Gospel: Decoding the Ancient Text that Reveals Jesus' Marriage to Mary the Magdalene, written by Simcha Jacobovici and Barrie Wilson (released November 12, 2014) is a book that provides the first ever translation, from Syriac into English, of this unique document that tells the inside story of Jesus' social, family and political life.

Taking the reader on an unparalleled historical adventure through a paradigm shifting manuscript, what the authors eventually discover is as astounding as it is surprising: the confirmation of Jesus' marriage to Mary Magdalene; the names of their two children; the towering presence of Mary

Magdalene; a previously unknown plot on Jesus' life (thirteen years prior to the crucifixion); an assassination attempt against Mary Magdalene and their children; Jesus' connection to political figures at the highest level of the Roman Empire; and a religious movement that antedates that of Paul, namely, the Church of Mary Magdalene.

———————

Part historical detective story, part modern adventure, if their historical sleuthing is correct, this text is a Gospel *before* the Gospels, meaning that we can finally return Jesus to the historical context from which Paul removed him.

Barrie Wilson, Ph D [83]

Simcha Jacobovici [84]

———

[83] www.barriewilson.com
[84] blogs.timesofisrael.com/author/simcha-jacobovici/

Genealogy + Academia

What I find truly amazing about genealogy are the original documents that exist with which to further corroborate one's heritage; the French kept exceptional records.

The Fleur-de-Lis, also known as the *Lily of France*, is a symbol that has become associated with Mary Magdalene.

Aside from the Rose, I have always wondered why the Lily was always my second favorite flower; mayhap there was something in my subconscious, waiting to be freed.

Heraldic histories claim that it originated in the 10th century as a symbol of sovereignty, to be later adopted by King Louis VII as his personal emblem.

In truth, this symbol is one that has been found to go much further back in history, as far back as Assyrian ornamental design; so, too, has it also been depicted on Greek, Rome and Celtic coinage.

In France, its actual usage may well date back to the Merovingian King Clovis I, who purportedly wore an Iris flower in his helmet before riding off to battle.

Some associate this very symbol with a secret family line, carried by the Merovingian kings.

I am quickly coming to the realization there is no such thing as historical fact, only historical observation; subsequently *all history is comprised of as much opinion as fact and, in many cases, has been entirely fabricated for the furthering of the author's personal ambitions or secret agenda.* [85]

I am also learning that critical thinking, creative thinking and critical literacy are all important and key facets of this soul searching via text phenomenon.

Critical thinking involves logical thinking and reasoning, including skills such as comparison, classification, sequencing, cause/effect, patterning, webbing, analogies, deductive reasoning, inductive reasoning, forecasting, planning, hypothesizing and critiquing, of the so-called left brain.

---

[85] McGowan, Kathleen. (2006). The Expected One (page 22). New York, NY: Touchstone.

Creative thinking involves creating something new or original, the aim of which is to stimulate curiosity and promote divergence. Such involves the use of a multitude of skills such as flexibility, originality, fluency, elaboration, brainstorming, modification, imagery, associative thinking, attribute listing and metaphorical thinking, right brain activities.

Critical literacy pertains to the reader understanding the relationships that exist between their ideas and those presented by the author of the text by focusing on issues of power that promote reflection, action and transformation.

As per my Masters of Education (Literacy) program, according to Allan Luke and Peter Freebody and their Four Resources Model, [86] readers play not only the role of code breakers, meaning makers and text users, but also the role of text critics.

---

[86] Department of Education - Tasmania. (2006). *The Four Resources Model*. Retrieved March 8, 2007, from http://www.ltag.education.tas.gov.au/focus/beingliterate/FourResources.htm

Unfortunately, it is very difficult to be critical of an epoch of events that transpired well before you were born.

❖

Why should it come as a shocking surprise that Jesus and Mary Magdalene might well have been married?

In many of the Gospels, Jesus is referred to as a rabbi or teacher.

There are those who say that this speaks very strongly to his marital status, in that Mishnaic law (the collection of oral laws compiled about 200 AD by Rabbi Judah ha-Nasi that form the basic part of the Talmud) demands that a rabbi should take a wife because *an unmarried man may not be a teacher*.

In keeping, the idea that Jesus may have wed and, as a husband, sired children, is really not as controversial as it sounds.

In reference to direct ancestors living 40 generations ago (about the year 1000 AD), Douglas Rohde, Steve Olson and Joseph Chang have shared that this ancestral group included many millions of people.

Almost everyone living today had ancestors in Europe, Asia and Africa, and many present day Asians, Europeans and Africans had ancestors in the Americas because of the continual exchange of mates across the Bering Strait. [87]

Clearly, this means that *you and I are descended from all of the Africans, Australians, Native Americans and Europeans who were alive three millenniums ago and still have descendants living today. That's also why so many people living today could be descended from Jesus.* [88]

---

[87] Rohde, Douglas, Olson, Steve and Chang, Joseph. (2004, September 30). "Modelling the recent common ancestry of all living humans" article. *Nature, 431, 562-566.* Retrieved March 8, 2007
https://www.nature.com/articles/nature02842
[88] Ibid.

In conclusion, Steve shares that *people may like to think that they're descended from some ancient group while other people are not. But human ancestry doesn't work that way, since we all shared the same ancestors just a few millenniums ago. As that idea becomes more widely accepted, arguments over who's descended from Jesus won't result in lawsuits. And maybe, just maybe, people will have one less reason to feel animosity toward other branches of the human family.* [89]

These may well prove to be the truest words spoken to date.

---

[89] Rohde, Douglas, Olson, Steve and Chang, Joseph. (2004, September 30). "Modelling the recent common ancestry of all living humans" article. *Nature, 431, 562-566.* Retrieved March 8, 2007
https://www.nature.com/articles/nature02842

Cathars

During the early formation of what would later come to be known as Christianity, church authorities (known as Fathers of the Church of Rome) exerted considerable influence (energy) in weeding out what they termed *false* doctrine and yet in the words of Saint Bernard of Clairveaux, the Cathars were described thusly ......

If you interrogate them, no one could be more Christian. As to their conversation, nothing can be less reprehensible, and what they speak, they prove by deeds. As for the morals of the heretics, they cheat no one, they oppress no one, they strike no one. [90]

The Cathars claimed to possess a secret <u>Book of Love</u>, a gospel of Jesus (Yeshua), written not in words, but in

---

[90] Freke, Timothy, and Gandy, Peter. (2001) <u>Jesus and The Lost Goddess: The Secret Teachings of the Original Christians</u> (page 84). Three Rivers Press: New York, New York.

symbols derived from a very ancient tradition; a book that was given to John the Divine.

The existence of this lost (or hidden) gospel, the foundation of the Cathar Church of Love (or Amor, the total reversal of Roma, meaning Rome), was revealed when the Church subjected the Cathars to torture; likewise, during the torturing of the Templar Knights in 1308.

The Cathars, aware of the laws of Duality, were adepts at the transmutation of darkness through love and purity. It was their belief that man participates in God's victory toward ignorance (the absence of Light) and evil (the absence of Love); as a result, they taught internal alchemy, meaning the transmutation of the physical self into Gold (Golden Light).

The contents of the Book of Love involved a secret skill (symbolized by the Templar skull) said to both grant one the ability to control the forces of nature as well as to transform human blood into that of the wise, holy and pure blood of life equated with the Holy Grail. The point was to know the Grail, not as a cup, but as a transformation process from homo sapien into a pure one.

While the writings of the Cathars have, for the most part, been destroyed, because of the doctrinal threat as perceived by the Papacy, there are a few texts that were preserved by their opponents.

The *Rituel Cathare de Lyon* provides us with a mere glimpse of the inner working of their faith.

A Latin manuscript, *The Book of Two Principles*, kept in Florence, is "a translation made in 1260 from a work by the Cathar Jean de Lugio from Bergamo (written in 1230)." [91]

This Latin translation, found in Prague in 1939, came from an anonymous treaty written in Languedoc at the beginning of the 13th century." [92] It is conceivable that the author may have been the Parfait Barthelemy of Carcassonne.

---

[91] The Books by Gilles C. H. Nullens accessed on April 25, 2011 at https://nullens.org/catholics-heretics-and-heresy/part-1-the-cathars/1-2-introduction-to-the-cathar-religion-2/
[92] Ibid.

In reference to the area referred to as the Languedoc, word was sent "to the Pope that the Cathars were so inter-married into the local population of the region that it was impossible to identify who were Cathars and who weren't." [93]

When asked how the Crusaders would be able to discern the difference, the words uttered by Arnaud Amoury, the Cistercian Abbott of Citeaux, were *Caedite eos ... Novit enim Dominus qui sunt eius* ... meaning *Kill them all. God will recognize his own.* [94] [95]

The Albigensian Heresy was "melded around the Jewish Messianic Bloodline of Jesus that Rome so desperately sought to suppress, and this goes a long way towards explaining the Church's fanatical, unprecedented savagery against the peaceful and non-threatening Cathars." [96]

---

[93] Vayro, Ian Ross. (2007) <u>God Save Us From Religion</u> (page 188). Queensland, Australia: Joshua Books.
[94] https://en.wikipedia.org/wiki/Catharism
[95] www.cathar.info/120502_arnaud.htm
[96] Vayro, Ian Ross. (2007) <u>God Save Us From Religion</u> (page 188). Queensland, Australia: Joshua Books.

Aside from ideological disputes, the fast spread of Catharism in the 13th century "meant a painfully growing *loss of land and influence*. If allowed to continue, the impact of Catharism would have re-defined the fabric of medieval society. To protect the existing power base, the inquisition had been formed to get rid of the Cathars, by means of their complete genocide. Their democracy and Christ-like lifestyles had been considered an example too dangerous to allow even a trace of it to remain. The Christian Church, to date, proudly claims the brutal murder of unarmed Cathar men, women and children whose "fault" had been their sincere desire to live according to the values of Christ, to be its most significant victory." [97]

The traditional death toll, in the war against the Cathars, has been cited as over one million, as per the following sources: [1] John M. Robertson, <u>A Short History of Christianity</u> (London: Watts, 1902) p. 254; [2] Christopher Brookmyre, <u>Not the End of the World</u> (New York: Grove Press, 1998) p. 39; [3] Max Dimont, <u>Jews, God, and History</u> (New York:

---

[97] www.dhaxem.com/the_cathars.htm

Penguin, 1994) p. 225; [4] Dizerega Gus, Pagans and Christians: The Personal Spiritual Experience (St. Paul, MN: Llewellyn, 2001) p. 195; [5] Helen Ellerbe, The Dark Side of Christian History (Orlando, FL: Morningstar & Lark, 1995) p. 74, and [6] Michael Newton, Holy Homicide (Port Townsend, WA: Loompanics Unlimited, 1998) p. 117. [98]

We know that the Albigensian Crusades were aimed at eradicating a population, merely because they did not conform to the traditions of the RCC.

We also know that it was a conflict that "quickly devolved into a political war of conquest and land seizure." [99]

The Church of Rome (later known as the Roman Catholic Church) savagely attacked the Cathars of Southern France; they attacked with a viciousness that would later show itself paralleled in the atrocities committed, against the Jews, during World War II.

---

[98] necrometrics.com/pre1700a.htm
[99] deremilitari.org/2018/04/the-albigensian-crusade-a-comparative-military-study-1209-1218/

With Catharism threatening "the very existence, ubiquity and legitimacy of the Catholic Church," [100] this was naught but political and religious genocide, inflicted on a peaceable Christian people, taking place over the course of forty years (1209 to 1244).

Define Cathars [101]

---

[100] deremilitari.org/2018/04/the-albigensian-crusade-a-comparative-military-study-1209-1218/
[101] https://cathar.askdefine.com/

Women as Healers

Healing has always been regarded as the responsibility of mothers and wives.

As autonomous healers, women often were the only healers for other women as well as the poor; as midwives, they travelled from home to home and village to village.

The wise woman had a host of remedies which had been tested in years of use (with many developed herbal remedies still having their place in modern pharmacology); they had pain-killers, digestive aids and anti-inflammatory agents. [102]

As an empiricist, the wise woman relied on her senses (rather than on faith or doctrine), believing in trial and error, cause and effect. [103]

102

https://www.marxists.org/subject/women/authors/ehrenreich-barbara/witches.htm

[103] Ibid.

As an active inquirer, she trusted her ability to find ways to deal with disease, pregnancy and childbirth; in short, her magic was the science of her time. [104]

Unfortunately, these healers, deemed witches and charlatans by the authorities, became the target of witch hunting, a program of ruthless persecution. [105]

In the eyes of the RCC, the power of the witch was derived from her sexuality.

Empiricism and sexuality both represent a surrender to the senses, an ultimate and total betrayal of faith.

This, then, made the witch a triple threat to the RCC: [1] she was a woman, and not ashamed of it, [2] she appeared to be part of an organized underground of peasant women, and

---

[104]

https://www.marxists.org/subject/women/authors/ehrenreich-barbara/witches.htm
[105]

https://www.ncbi.nlm.nih.gov/pmc/articles/PMC1694293/ (page 288)

[3] she was a healer whose practice was based in empirical study. [106]

Practicing between earth and heaven as herbal healers, homeopathic healers, midwives, Priestesses, shaman and wise women, skills such as these afforded women both knowledge as well as power.

This is why women were persecuted as healers; hence, the witch hunts. Quite simply, it was the suppression of witches in medieval Europe that led to the rise of the male medical profession.

Now for the interesting segment.

The Church associated women with sex, and all pleasure in sex was condemned, because it could only come from the devil. Lust, then, in either man or wife, was blamed on the female.

---

[106]

https://www.marxists.org/subject/women/authors/ehrenreich
-barbara/witches.htm

Having been deemed weak vessels, and told that God created man first, women were made to feel less in his eyes, and yet theirs was the responsibility of bearing new life to the glory of God.

———————————◆———————————

Aztec Women: Capable Partners and Cosmic Enemies [107]

Female Shamanism, Goddess Cultures and Psychedelics [108]

Forgotten Women: Witches, Healers and Medicine Women [109]

Lessons of History: The Suppression of Women Healers 1 [110]

———————————

[107] www.mexicolore.co.uk/aztecs/home/aztec-women
[108] www.motherpeace.com/karen_female_shamanism.html
[109] https://www.huffingtonpost.com/gerit-quealy/forgotten-women-witches-h_b_859230.html
[110] zoebrooks.blogspot.ca/2012/06/lessons-of-history-suppression-of-women.html

Lessons of History: The Suppression of Women Healers 2 [111]

Medieval Attitudes about Women [112]

New Research shows that ancient Maya Women were Powerful Leaders [113]

Practicing between Heaven and Earth: Women Healers in Seventeenth Century Bologna [114]

The Lived Experience of Ojibwa and Cree Women Healers [115]

---

[111] zoebrooks.blogspot.ca/2012/07/lessons-of-history-suppression-of-women.html
[112] https://www.slideshare.net/jm10492/medieval-attitudes-about-women
[113] https://www.sott.net/article/242682-New-research-shows-ancient-Maya-women-were-powerful-leaders
[114] https://www.raco.cat/index.php/Dynamis/article/viewFile/106145/150121
[115] https://www.ncbi.nlm.nih.gov/pubmed/11847813

The Persecution of Women as Healers [116]

The Vulnerability of Women to Witchcraft Accusations [117]

Traditional Witchcraft is Medical Heresy: The Patriarchal Medical Establishment versus Witches as Healers [118]

<u>Witches, Midwives and Nurses: A History of Women Healers</u> [119] [120]

Woman Shaman [121]

---

[116] www.tamarawolfson.com/historical-perspective-women-as-healers.html

[117] https://www.salemtarot.com/archive/seminar.html

[118]

https://traditionalwitchcraftandoccultism.wordpress.com/tag/women-as-healers/

[119] https://muse.jhu.edu/books/9781558616905

[120] https://www.feministes-radicales.org/wp-content/uploads/2012/06/Barbara-Ehrenreich-and-Deirdre-English-Witches-Midwives-and-Nurses-A-History-of-Women-Healers.-Introduction..pdf

[121] www.suppressedhistories.net/articles/womanshaman.html

Women and Medicine [122]

Women and Medicine in the Middle Ages and Renaissance [123]

Women and the Practice of Medical Care in Early Modern Europe, 1400 to 1800 [124]

Women Healers and the Medieval Church [125]

Women Healers of the Middle Ages: Selected Aspects of Their History [126]

---

[122] www.oxfordbibliographies.com/view/document/obo-9780195399301/obo-9780195399301-0278.xml
[123] www.gallowglass.org/jadwiga/herbs/WomenMed.html
[124] https://www.palgrave.com/us/book/9780230282919
[125] http://www.witch.plus.com/7day-extracts/women-healers.html
[126]

http://www.ncbi.nlm.nih.gov/pmc/articles/PMC1694293/pdf/amjph00539-0138.pdf

Women Healers Past and Present: An Historical View of Women in Medicine from Earliest Times to Today [127]

Women's Healing Art: Domestic Medicine in the Turn-of-the-Century Ozarks [128]

Women, Health and Healing in Early Modern Europe [129]

Women in Medicine: Priestesses and Healers or Second-Class Doctors? [130]

---

[127] https://www.ontheissuesmagazine.com/1992spring/levin_spring1992.php

[128] beckerexhibits.wustl.edu/mowihsp/articles/Ozarks.htm

[129] www.academia.edu/2944294/Women_Health_and_Healing_in_Early_Modern_Europe

[130] archive.samj.org.za/1997%20VOL%2087%20Jan-Dec/9-12/Articles/11%20November/11.3%20WOMEN%20IN%20MEDICINE%20-%20PRIESTESSES%20AND%20HEALERS%20OR%20SECOND-CLASS%20DOCTORS.%20Jocelyn%20Kane-Berman.pdf

Malleus Maleficarum

Magic, sorcery, and witchcraft had long been condemned by the Church; their attitude towards witchcraft, as explained in the canon Episcopi (written in about 900 AD), [131] stated that witchcraft and magic did not really exist, and that those who believed in such things "had been seduced by the Devil in dreams and visions into old pagan errors." [132] [133]

Until about 1400, it was rare for anyone to be accused of witchcraft, despite the fact that heresies had become a major problem within the Church by the 13th century. By the 15th century, belief in witches was widely accepted in European society, their persecution becoming more brutal following the publication of the Malleus Maleficarum; it was clear that witchcraft had become accepted as both real and dangerous.

---

[131] https://en.wikipedia.org/wiki/Canon_Episcopi
[132] Pavlac, Brian (2010). Witch Hunts in the Western World: Persecution and Punishment from the Inquisition through the Salem Trials (page 29). Bison Books: Lincoln, NB.
[133] staff.kings.edu/bapavlac/

In 1484, Heinrich Kramer, a German Catholic clergyman, had made one of the first attempts at prosecuting alleged witches in the Tyrol region; not successful, he was expelled from the city of Innsbruck and dismissed by the local bishop as a "senile old man." [134]

Kramer was opposed by the local clergy partly because of his eccentric behavior (as the Bishop of Innsbruck's verdict indicates), and partly because he did not hold any official position as an Inquisitor, despite his efforts to make himself into one. [135] According to Diarmaid MacCulloch, the writing of Malleus Maleficarum (commonly rendered into English as Hammer of [the] Witches) was Kramer's act of self-justification and revenge.

Summis Desiderantes Affectibus, a Papal Bull decreed by Pope Innocent VIII on December 5, 1484, addresses the presence of witchcraft in Germany and in other areas; this bull was published as part of the preface of the book,

[134] https://en.wikipedia.org/wiki/Malleus_Maleficarum
[135] Ibid.

implying papal approval for the work. [136] [137] The bull urged local authorities to cooperate with the inquisitors and threatened those who impeded their work with excommunication. [138] [139] Despite this threat, the bull failed to ensure that Kramer got the support he wanted.

Some scholars view the bull as clearly political, motivated by jurisdictional disputes between the local German Catholic priests and clerics from the Office of the Inquisition who answered more directly to the pope. [140]

In 1490, three years after its publication, the Catholic Church condemned the Malleus Maleficarum, although it was later used by royal courts during the Renaissance, and

---

[136] https://sourcebooks.fordham.edu/source/witches1.asp
[137]
https://en.wikipedia.org/wiki/Summis_desiderantes_affectib us
[138] Darst, David H. (October 15, 1979). "Witchcraft in Spain: The Testimony of Martín de Castañega's Treatise on Superstition and Witchcraft (1529)." Proceedings of the American Philosophical Society 123 (5): 298–322
[139] http://www.jstor.org/discover/10.2307/986592 (page 299)
[140] Ibid, page 298.

contributed to the increasingly brutal prosecution of witchcraft during the 16th and 17th centuries.

The preface also includes an approbation from the University of Cologne's Faculty of Theology; even if the endorsement were genuine, it was misrepresented by Kramer, as was the copy of *Summis Desiderantes Affectibus*, a bull issued *before* the Malleus Maleficarum was written.

A most successful advertising strategy, Kramer did not even need the approval of the Cologne University theologians; for good measure, however, Institoris forged a document granting their apparently unanimous approbation. [141] The letter of Pope Innocent VIII was not an approval of the book, to which it was appended, but rather a charge to inquisitors to investigate diabolical sorcery and a warning to those who might impede them in their duty. [142]

----

[141] https://en.wikipedia.org/wiki/Malleus_Maleficarum (citation 17)
[142] https://en.wikipedia.org/wiki/Malleus_Maleficarum (citation 16)

It is doubtful whether either Pope Innocent VIII or the theological faculty of Cologne actually read the <u>Malleus Maleficarum</u> document. In truth, the <u>Malleus Maleficarum</u> was simply another means with which to further discredit and subjugate women.

❊

Malleus Maleficarum (online and downloadable scan of original Latin edition of 1490) [143]

Malleus Maleficarum (online version of Latin text and scanned pages of version published in 1580) [144]

Professor Pavlac's Witch Hunts [145]

---

[143] diglib.hab.de/inkunabeln/151-quod-2f-1/start.htm
[144] ebooks.library.cornell.edu/cgi/t/text/text-idx?c=witch;cc=witch;view=toc;subview=short;idno=wit060
[145] www.brianpavlac.org/witchhunts/index.html

Terror of History: Mystics, Heretics, and Witches in the Western Tradition course (Professor Teofilo F. Ruiz, University of California at Los Angeles) [146]

---

[146] https://www.thegreatcourses.com/courses/terror-of-history-mystics-heretics-and-witches-in-the-western-tradition.html

Women in the Early Church

The Bible tells us that women were the last disciples at the cross and the first at the empty tomb, and yet one of the best-kept secrets in Christianity is the significant and strategic role that women played in the early church. [147] [148] The question that bodes asking is, quite frankly, a simple and unadorned one ... why the secret?

Professor Kate Cooper of the University of Manchester has identified dozens of forgotten Christian women who were influential in the first and second centuries, during a period when Christianity was, in some respects, more progressive towards women than today. [149]

---

[147] https://www.bild.org/download/summit/Women-Spontaneous-Expansion.pdf

[148] http://commons.emich.edu/cgi/viewcontent.cgi?article=1064&context=honors

[149] www.dailymail.co.uk/sciencetech/article-2390252/Women-airbrushed-early-Christianity-despite-having-crucial-spread-claims-leading-historian.html

She believes that women played a central role in spreading the new Christian faith through informal friendship and family networks.

Given the distinction that existed between the sexes in the first century, the fact that there arose a need for women elders to counsel, and instruct, the congregation should come as no surprise. [150] [151]

We know that women played an important role, both in Jesus' ministry as well as in the spread of Christianity. The following list contains just a few of the valuable spiritual contributions women have made in the history of the church.

→Mary and Martha were close friends of Jesus. (Luke 10:38-39)

→Mary anointed Jesus prior to his death. (John 12:3)

150

https://christianhistoryinstitute.org/magazine/article/women-in-the-early-church
151

https://www.pbs.org/wgbh/pages/frontline/shows/religion/first/women.html

→Many women lamented Jesus' crucifixion. (Luke 23:27-31 and John 19:25)

→Women were the first to visit Jesus' tomb on Resurrection morning. (Luke 23:55-24:1)

→Early church leaders responded positively to the complaints of widows. (Acts 6:1-6)

→Dorcas was "abounding with deeds of kindness and charity" throughout her community; when Peter later raised her from the dead, many townspeople believed in Christ. (Acts 9:36-42)

→The church gathered in Mary's home to pray for Peter. (Acts 12:12)

→Women gathered for worship at Philippi, where Paul spoke to them. (Acts 16:13)

→Lydia was a successful businesswoman; she became a Christian and prevailed upon Paul and his colleagues to meet in her home. (Acts 16:14-15)

→In Thessalonica, "a number of the leading women" were responsive to Paul and Silas' teaching. (Acts 17:4)

→In Berea, many "believed, along with a number of prominent Greek women." (Acts 17:12)

→Priscilla and Aquila, her husband, were partners in church work. (Acts 18:2 and 18:19)

→Both Priscilla and Aquila corrected Apollo's theology. (Acts 18:26)

→Paul mention Phoebe as a "servant of the church … a helper of many and myself." (Romans 16:1)

→Paul calls Priscilla "a fellow worker." (Romans 16:3)

→ "Chloe's people" gave Paul information on the Corinthian problems. (1 Corinthians 1:11)

→Paul lets unmarried women "stay as they are" so they can serve the Lord and not be forced into marriage. (1 Corinthians 7:28)

→Widows were given special attention, assistance and care. (1 Timothy 5:3-6)

―――――✖―――――

Courtesy of my research, it soon became evident to me that one of the greatest failures of so-called organized religion involves the disempowerment and mistreatment of women. In fact, the seed of misogyny (the hatred or dislike of women or girls) was *implanted in the Christian psyche by the Bible.* [152] [153]

When Emperor Constantine converted to Christianity in 313 AD, the religion became institutionalized with *male* bishops and members of clergy.

In fact it was Augustine who elevated the hatred of women (and sex) to a level unsurpassed before, stating the inferiority of women to men, further concluding that woman was created purely for procreation; furthermore, it was

___

[152] www.geocities.ws/paulntobin/womenfathers.html
[153] www.geocities.ws/paulntobin/womenbible.html

sexual pleasure that carried the original sin from generation to generation. [154]

As a result, sexual relations for purposes aside from procreation was deemed mortally sinful while sexual relations for procreation, while still sinful, was deemed pardonable.

Augustine also blamed women for the fall from grace.

When Augustine wrote <u>On The Trinity</u>, [155] he tried to work out a conundrum (a confusing and difficult problem or question); he wanted to figure out how women could be held to be the image of God.

He solved the puzzle by writing that *when a woman is alone, then she is not in the image of God; it is only when she is joined with a man, when she is one flesh with him, that she can be considered the image of God.* [156]

---

[154] www.geocities.ws/paulntobin/womenfathers.html
[155] www.newadvent.org/fathers/130112.htm
[156] https://www.redletterchristians.org/sex-pills-image-god/

So, when the woman becomes one flesh with the man, it can be said that she represents the image of God and yet to engage in sexual relations for purposes aside from procreation was deemed mortally sinful.

With an emphasis on sexuality as the root of all evil, such was simply a means with which to further subordinate all women.

One can only conclude that Christian theology has been, from its very beginning, a theology of hatred of women; a theology that was acted upon when Christianity became the dominant force in the Roman empire. [157]

The position of women, in the west, has only improved in recent years, mainly due to the decline in the temporal power of the churches; however, even today this tradition of misogyny continues to express itself in the staunch opposition of the Catholic church to abortion and birth control. [158]

---

[157] www.geocities.ws/paulntobin/womenfathers.html
[158] Ibid.

To further share the words of Lilly Cruz, as a means of further reflection ... *In the <u>Genesis</u> account of creation, we read how God created both men and women. Women are of equal value in God's eyes. Although men and women are created for different purposes and as many psychologists can attest, have different thinking patterns, women were meant to be an integral part of humanity and have purpose and significance in God's creation and purpose. If not, why would God ignore half of the population He created?*

———————✄———————

5 Women of the Early Church You Should Know [159]

An Adventure in Confusion on Women as Bishops and Priests [160] [161]

———————————————

[159] https://www.redletterchristians.org/5-women-early-church-know/
[160] https://gracetracer.wordpress.com/2012/04/11/an-adventure-in-confusion-on-women-as-bishops-and-priests/
[161] https://rachelheldevans.com/blog/women-of-the-passion-links

The Neglected History of Women in the Early Church [162]

The Position of Women: The Teachings of the Theologians [163]

The Position of Women: The Historical Consequences [164]

The Power and Presence of Women in the Earliest Churches [165]

The Role of Women (According to Jesus and the Early Church) [166]

The Roles For Women [167]

---

[162]
https://www.christianhistoryinstitute.org/magazine/article/women-in-the-early-church/

[163] www.geocities.ws/paulntobin/womenfathers.html

[164] www.geocities.ws/paulntobin/women.html

[165] https://www.huffingtonpost.com/greg-carey/women-in-the-earliest-churches_b_985526.html

[166] www.womenpriests.org/classic/karris2.asp

[167]
https://www.pbs.org/wgbh/pages/frontline/shows/religion/first/roles.html

The Story of God: Women in the Early Church [168]

Unveiling Precedent: Reclaiming the Power of Women in the Early Church [169]

When Women Were Priests: Women's Leadership in the Early Church and the Scandal of Their Subordination in the Rise of Christianity [170]

Women and the Early Churches [171]

Women and the Spontaneous Expansion of the Early Church [172]

---

[168] godswordtowomen.org/walford2.htm
[169] http://commons.emich.edu/cgi/viewcontent.cgi?article=1064&context=honors
[170] https://www.amazon.com/exec/obidos/ASIN/0060686618/
[171] store.fortresspress.com/media/downloads/0800638263_Chapter1.pdf
[172] https://www.bild.org/download/summit/Women-Spontaneous-Expansion.pdf

Women have been airbrushed out of early Christianity, despite having been crucial to its spread, claims leading historian [173]

Women in the Earliest Churches [174]

Women in the Early Church [175]

Women in the Early Christian Church [176]

Women's Vital Role in Early Church Should Be Restored [177]

---

[173] https://www.dailymail.co.uk/sciencetech/article-2390252/Women-airbrushed-early-Christianity-despite-having-crucial-spread-claims-leading-historian.html
[174] catdir.loc.gov/catdir/samples/cam034/87024916.pdf
[175] www.patheos.com/blogs/jesuscreed/2013/09/25/women-in-the-early-church/
[176]

www.angelmessage.org/women_in_the_early_christian_chu rch.htm
[177] https://www.belfasttelegraph.co.uk/opinion/news-analysis/womens-vital-role-in-early-church-should-be-restored-28736007.html

Gnostic Sophia, Divine Feminine

During both the Crusades, as well as the Inquisition, anyone who was proven to be a heretic (meaning that they believed outside the dictates of the RCC) was killed; as a result, most Gnostic traditions went underground and continued to operate in secret.

While some traditions died out, others continued; everything was dependant on the ability to stay hidden and train initiates.

Sophian Gnosticism claims its tradition comes directly from Saint Mary Magdalene; the Apostle of the Apostles and the first to see the risen Christ.

In accordance with the Introduction to Sophian Gnosticism Study Guide,[178] there is much that I have learned, namely,

---

[178] http://www.magdalene-circle.org/Sophian_Gnostic_Tradition_Study_Guide.pdf

[1] In the New Testament it is said that the name of Yeshua has power and can banish dark and unclean spirits.

In Hebrew, Yeshua is spelled Yod Heh Shin Vav Heh; very similar to the divine name of God, YHWH, which is spelled Yod Heh Vav Heh.

More a designation than a name, YHWH means *that which was, is and forever shall be.* This can be taken to indicate a divine being, but it also means a force or the life power.

In keeping, then, the name Yeshua literally translates to *YHWH delivers* or *the truth will set you free.*

The Shin in Yeshua's name is very significant because it most often refers to the Holy Spirit (or Shekinah); the power and presence of God within and beyond creation.

This further implies that (a) the name Yeshua signifies an embodiment of this consciousness force, and that (b) Gnosis comes by embodying this force.

[2] The willingness to seek direct spiritual experience, the foundation of all mystical traditions, lies at the heart of Sophian Gnosticism.

This knowledge (or wisdom) is secret (or hidden from view) because one cannot speak about the inner teachings; they have to be experienced to be understood.

Gnosis is not limited by God or man, but by the individual and their desire for the spiritual experience.

Gnosis, then, is knowledge acquired through direct spiritual (mystical) experience of God; each becomes the *living* Gnosis, the word made manifest, so to speak.

[3] From the Gnostic perspective, the purpose of one's incarnation is the revelation of what (who) they truly are; a revelation that helps us to see the image of our true selves, thereby empowering us to activate our divine potential.

From this viewpoint, Yeshua does not come to redeem us from sin, but rather to redeem us from cosmic ignorance, thereby imparting true Gnosis.

[4] According to the Kabbalah, the first human soul, Adam Kadmon, was an androgynous being.

Having been created in the image and likeness of God, we can interpret this to mean that God is also an androgynous being.

With Adam having been divided into male and female, both said to be in the likeness of God, this division speaks of both the *male and female aspects of consciousness* as well as the *male and female aspects of the divine being*.

[5] Sophian tradition does speak of a trinity, but more often of a tetrad consisting of Father, Mother, Son and Daughter.

This is further reflected in the divine name Yahweh which consists of the Hebrew letters Yah, Heh, Vav, Heh.

The Yah is considered God the Father, the first Heh is God the Mother, the Vav is God the Son, and the second Heh is God the Daughter (or Bride).

The Father (Yahweh) is considered the transcendent form of the divine, the force of divine power.

The Mother (Elohim) is the imminent aspect of the divine, the matrix of the life-power in many forms.

[6] In addressing both the Father and Mother, they do not mean to imply that they are speaking of a God and a Goddess, but of masculine and feminine aspects of the One God, represented as *both* Mother and Father.

[7] The second coming of Christ is not the same for a Sophian as for a traditional Christian.

Sophians do not consider Yeshua to be the only Christed individual. As a result, the coming of the Christos can occur for anyone as they reach enlightenment and supernal consciousness; hence, the second coming is a personal experience for the individual.

[8] Many Gnostics have noticed the difference in tone and texture between the Old and New Testaments of the Christian Bible; this has led many to believe that there is a different God that is spoken of between the two.

The Sethian Gnostic tradition (among other dualistic Gnostic schools) attributes the Old Testament to the Demiurge and the New Testament to the True God.

The Sophian tradition states that they do not believe that it is God that changes between the Testaments, but that the people, themselves, are the ones that have changed; as a result, they see the difference as a spiritual evolution of the people.

When Sophian Gnostics look at scriptures, they see a progressive light transmission occurring at various levels, each more refined and evolved from the last. In keeping, they look to draw whatever spiritual wisdom they can, leaving anything obsolete behind.

In the Gnostic tradition, Sophia is a powerful female figure of Wisdom; one of the feminine aspects of God.

Wherein her origins seem impossible to trace, scholars have suggested [1] Semitic sources (the goddess of love and fertility, Ishtar), [2] Egyptian sources (Maat, the goddess of conception), and [3] Hellenistic sources (the goddesses

Demeter, Persephone, Hecate, and Isis), finding no source for Sophia within the Hebrew tradition, they have dated Sophia's textual sources at least 500 years after most of the Hebrew tradition was developed. [179]

Sophia = Wisdom = feminine

Christos = Logos = masculine

In referencing Sophia, then, we are really speaking of the feminine aspect of the Divine, the feminine aspect of Christos, and the feminine aspect of ourselves.

Both need to become merged to experience the wholeness of our divinity; it becomes through this balance and unification of the masculine and feminine that the male and female are actualized and made complete.

---

[179]

https://www2.kenyon.edu/Depts/Religion/Projects/Reln91/Gender/Gnosticism.htm

This union of masculine and feminine principles, within the Sophian teachings, is understood inwardly, within oneself, as a *sacred marriage* of the male and female aspects of ourselves on both psychic and spiritual levels. [180]

The psychic level marriage results in one's true intelligence and creativity being expressed; in comparison, the spiritual level marriage results in the union of the heavenly and earthly aspects of our soul of Light through which we experience various states of higher consciousness or divine illumination. [181] Eventually, however, Sophia was completely fused with Christ.

In her essay, "Wisdom Was Made Flesh and Pitched Her Tent Among Us," [182] Elizabeth A. Johnson argues that the feminine Wisdom was replaced by the masculine Logos *as it became unseemly, given the developing patriarchal*

---

[180] www.llewellyn.com/journal/article/659
[181] Ibid.
[182] Stevens, Maryanne. (1993) <u>Reconstructing the Christ Symbol: Essays in Feminist Christology</u> (page 105). Eugene, OR: Wipf and Stock Publishers.

tendencies in the church, to interpret the male Jesus with a female symbol of God. [183]

The authors of <u>Wisdom's Feast</u>, however, offer a very different theory; they have suggested that in order to recognize Jesus as an equal to God the Father, all explicit associations between Jesus and the weaker Sophia had to be abandoned. [184]

183

https://www2.kenyon.edu/Depts/Religion/Projects/Reln91/Gender/Gnosticism.htm
[184] Ibid.

My Search Continued

What was I searching for? There was no face; there was no body. It was not until reading <u>The Woman with the Alabaster Jar: Mary Magdalene and the Holy Grail</u>, many years later, that I was able to identify the object of my search; that of the Divine Feminine.

I began pouring over books on Wicca and Goddess spirituality, while also resonating most strongly with the philosophy as held by aboriginal peoples with respect to Mother Earth.

One book would continue to lead me to another; there were so many books, that I simply cannot remember where it was that my search began. It was this manner of research that I was guided to explore my interest in crystals and alternative healing, eventually leading to the accumulation of a Crystal Healing Practitioner diploma as well as several Reiki certificates.

It has since become my personal philosophy to take what resonates from a multitude of sources, leaving behind what does not; as I continue to change, so does my frame of reference.

In keeping, I have become quite the eclectic and conglomerate mixture; seeking, challenging, and yet, above all, always resonating with my own inner truth.

Initially, I had been of the premise that love was all that was needed so as to enlighten one's self, thereby making the world a better place.

It was upon further reflection, meditation, reading and research, however, that I was most surprised to realize that although love is, and shall always be, a key piece of the cosmic puzzle, there is, in actual fact, a far more crucial piece that has been missing for sometime; namely, *ourselves*.

Caught up in the web of competition, greed, jealousy, envy and hate, we have been lost to ourselves for a very long time.

As the ultimate drivers, we have been asleep at the wheel for far too long; we have completely forgotten who we are.

In having done so, we have also forgotten how to celebrate the expanse and greatness of all life.

Knowing that I needed to awaken from my deep slumber, knowing that I needed to become more aware, as I rode off, on my stallion, in my search for the Divine Feminine, it had suddenly become clear that I was in search of myself.

It has always been my belief that the entirety of creation is sacred.

In remembering our connection to the entirety of creation, the challenge is to see the oneness, within the difference, that all share, while also enjoying the difference, the uniqueness, that makes life fascinating.

Everyone is endowed with the potential to create their own reality experience; most of us have been conditioned to look outside of ourselves for the answers.

We have allowed others to choose for us, to decide for us, to create for us; we have given them *carte blanche* power to dictate, to us, the reality of our experience. Is it not surprising, then, to discover that most are living the exact same dictated truth?

As the Buddha said, *you cannot do violence to another when you realize oneness.*

The key lies in listening to your inner being, discovering your reality from the inside, and thereafter directing your outward life in said manner.

As you begin to live according to your own guidance, daring to break free, you become further empowered; your emotions, then, are no longer entangled within the Matrix. By the Matrix, I am referring to those who create and dictate the reality for the greater multitude.

There have been times when I have been led to some rather controversial metaphysical material; all in good time, they say, for *when the student is ready, the teacher will appear.*

The Creation of Adam fresco (Sistine Chapel)

Does anyone recognize the woman on the right hand of God?

Until I discovered her identity to be Divine Wisdom, also known as Sophia, as depicted in the fresco on the Sistine Chapel ceiling by Michelangelo Buonarroti (1511), I had never encountered her before.

An embodiment of the Divine Feminine, Mary Magdalene has long been associated with Sophia (Wisdom).

Does not the Sistine Sophia encourage us to seek our inner wisdom from within the soul vault of knowingness as a means of reconnecting with the Divine Feminine?

I believe that she is the teacher we all seek.

The more I read, study and research, while on this spiritual journey, the more I am coming to realize that, quite honestly, I know naught what I thought I once knew; so much so that I am unable to pinpoint, at this time, what it is that I *believe* I know.

As most cleverly written by Thich Nhat Hanh ... *We must not be attached to a view or a doctrine, even a Buddhist one, for the Buddha said that if in a certain moment or place you adopt something as the absolute truth, and you attach to that, then you will no longer have any chance to reach the truth. Even when the truth comes and knocks on your door, and asks you to open the door, you won't recognize it. So you must not be too attached to dogma, to what you believe, and to what you perceive.*

It certainly seems that simplicity is best, doesn't it?

I have reached the threshold in my life whereby I am willing to consent that I know very little.

Perhaps the question that needs to be answered is ... *what is it that I think I know?*

My Understanding of Truth

It was the Roman church that usurped the reign of the Merovingian kings (the first major royal dynasty of what would eventually become France) who ruled by divine right, whilst creating the lineage that followed, known as the Carolingian kings.

Interestingly enough, the grandmother of Charlemagne was a Merovingian princess; namely, Bertrada of Prüm, daughter of King Thierry (Theuderic) III [185] and Clotilde dite Doda, and the sister to both Clovis IV and Clotaire IV.

This is the church that has both abused and misused power because they wanted to be in total control; anything that gave people power was forbidden. In addition, those who owned property held sway and control over all of those who did not.

185

fmg.ac/Projects/MedLands/MEROVINGIANS.htm#Theode ricIIIdied691

This is the church that sought to capture the mind and will of the populace.

This is the church that took a beautiful Truth and distorted it for their own nefarious purposes.

This is the church that granted indulgences to those who were looking for absolution of their sins, if they would but take on the mantle, take on the cloak, of those who would gladly, and eagerly, kill and maim others in the so-called name of God.

If anything was followed other than what they deemed should be followed, the Roman church (later referred to as the Catholic Church) persecuted all as heretics; in accordance with those who wielded the power, you were told only what they wanted you to know, be it information or disinformation.

This is the church that has abused, accused, controlled, dominated, interrogated, murdered and tortured humanity.

This is the church that has neglected to teach that all souls were One; that all souls were as connected to one another as they were to their Creator.

This is the church that has enforced guilty until proven innocent, and that seldom happened; as a result, people were constantly suspicious of their neighbors.

Knowing that the leaders of the church were constantly prodding people to come forth with the names of those among their midst who were not faithful followers, one simply did not divulge anything of a personal nature.

This is the church that taught separateness and selfishness, hatred and disconnectivity.

This is the church that instigated a brutal war of ignorance, a war wherein there was no safe place to hide.

This is the church that abhorred the sacredness of life, as was clearly evident in the creation of the concept of original sin.

This is the church that abhorred the sacredness of the female, those from whom life sprung, deeming sexuality to be evil, to be temptation, to be unclean.

Had either Apollonius of Tyana or Yeshua intended to establish a church, it would *never* have been one built on foundation principles such as these; to do that would have meant denying themselves and the tenets of truth (joy, love, peace) that were evident in their actions, in their acumen (insight), in their beliefs, in their teachings, in their words.

It is my personal belief that Yeshua was the son of God, just as every man and woman is also the son and daughter of God; all are created in the same fashion, all are an individuated spark of the Divine.

It is also my personal understanding that his soul was more evolved than that of the so-called ordinary man and woman; hence, he came as an avatar (meaning an embodiment or personification of a principle, an attitude, or a view of life) to the entirety of humanity.

It has become imperative that we take the time to see the Truth that exists in this world.

It has become imperative that we take the time to meditate on this Truth.

It has become imperative that we take the time to delve within, so as to better understand this Truth; in this way, each becomes both teacher and student.

As you come to understand the greater Truth, so, too, do you begin to understand the context in which you are to live your life, transcending the limitations that you have imposed (consciously or otherwise) upon yourself.

It has become imperative that we take the time to see that life is sacred, that life is to be lived, that life is to be enjoyed.

It has become imperative that we take the time to understand that in remaining true to one's self, to one's inner truth, so, too, are we remaining true to each other, including the Creator. This, then, becomes our means of liberation from the yoke of oppression, the yoke of enslavement, the yoke of captivity.

In truth, it matters naught to whom the universal principles of unconditional love and respect to all mankind belong; when followed, they bring peace, even to the most hardened of souls.

As well, it is equally important that we continue to allow others the right to their own thoughts, ideas and opinions without criticism, condemnation or persecution.

It is Spirit that concentrates on the essence of the message, as compared to organized religion, the man-made institution that concentrates its focus on the messenger, the profits, and total control over the lives of its believers. [186]

In truth, it all comes down to finding perfect peace, within yourself, and then using this same peace to create the much necessary, and needed, change for humanity, albeit courtesy of the example of how you life your life; in this way, you become a light, a beacon, unto others.

---

[186] https://hwarmstrong.com/enlyten-apollonius.htm

I am not here to please anyone, save myself.

I am not here to criticize.

I am not here to judge.

I am not here to condemn.

It is simply my job to *become that which I seek* and thereafter to continue to live my life in said manner whilst also engaging in that which I love to do, that which constitutes my passion.

I am here to live a life of joy.

I am here to live a life of passion.

I am here to live a life of wonder.

I am here to live a life of rediscovery.

I am here to live a life of Truth.

I am here to live a life of intuitive knowingness.

I am here to live a life of authenticity.

So, too, do I believe that you, the reader, are also here to live thusly.

There are certain universal laws of nature that govern our existence and guide our lives; the Law of Attraction is but one of these.

That having been said, life is a choice.

I choose to be positive.

I choose to be thankful for each and every day.

I choose to express gratitude.

I choose to become empowered by the truth of my own thoughts.

I choose to delve within to rediscover my truth.

I choose to celebrate life.

I choose to be happy.

I choose to be the best version of me that I can be.

I choose to be around the right people.

I choose to smile more often.

I choose to Let Go and Let God.

I choose to help others when I can.

I choose to be thankful for the life lessons that I have successfully mastered; so, too, do I choose to embrace the next step.

I choose to seek answers to my questions.

I choose to deliberate upon the answers that are received.

I choose to live a life of authenticity.

I choose to embrace a life of compassion.

I choose to live a life of compassionate allowing.

I choose to live a life of honesty.

I choose to live a life of truth.

I choose to allow others to live the life that they choose to live.

I choose to honor the private sanctuary of my mind, refusing to allow the negative beliefs of others to invade.

I choose to foster forgiveness so that all, including myself, may heal.

I choose to take control of my boundaries and what I allow myself to absorb from others.

I choose to engage in activities that are meaningful to me.

In accordance with the mystical traditions that came to be known as alchemy, many have looked at these processes as being about converting the physical metal of lead into gold, but the key message in all of this was the *transformation of the individual* and thereby discovering what it means to be spirit residing within a human (physical) body.

In essence, we are here to bring forth a new way of living as we work towards bringing Heaven down to Earth in the knowingness that all is One, that all is Love.

The physical body is actually *a doorway to a vast spiritual awakening, and we say this to you because the body enables humanity, through the balance of emotions, the balance of working through the mind, the brain, the endocrine system; all of these things line up in a certain way and use the chakra system to be able to access all knowledge in the Cosmos. And this is done through Kundalini and the ability to journey; the ability to take part of your consciousness and explore any area that you wish to explore, all the way up to Prime Creator in the Centre of the Cosmos. That's what your body is all about.* [187]

Clearly, this is the internal landscape that we are here to understand, to live, to employ.

---

[187] Presser, Dr. Richard and Evers, Carolyn. <u>True Stories of the Templar Knights</u> (page 82)

Planetary Energies

According to authors Monica Sjoo and Barbara Mor, it is written in <u>The Great Cosmic Mother</u>, that between the fifteenth and the eighteenth centuries alone, an estimated 1 to 9 million people, mostly women, were killed as pagan witches. [188] With the word witch meaning *wise woman* and the word pagan meaning *country dweller*, it appears, to me, that the male dominated church, in fear of losing its power, destroyed millions of women, many of them healers, herbalists, keepers of ancient customs and lores; in addition, the men opened medical schools and did not allow entry to women.[189]

Masculine energy is all about power, rationale and intellect (needing to do, needing to control).

---

[188] Briar, Kathy. *In Search of The Feminine Divine.* Retrieved March 8, 2007
www.gaiafriends.org/search.txt.html
[189] Ibid.

Feminine energy is all about feeling, knowing and intuition (simply BEing and allowing).

The planet, as a whole, has simply been basking in male energies for much too long.

It is only recently, if one looks at universal time, that the male and female energies have been "perceived" as being different, contrary, opposed. In fact, they are one. Our purpose here is to understand how this separation occurred, only so we can heal the gap and return to the oneness of creation that, in truth, has always been there. [190]

In bringing back the balance that once existed between our feminine and masculine aspects, such will enable all to become whole once again, for it is in the blending, balancing and harmonizing of both the Yin (feminine) and Yang (masculine), these compatible parts of ourselves, that we truly begin to experience the magnificent divine beings that we are.

---

[190] Briar, Kathy. *In Search of The Feminine Divine.* Retrieved March 8, 2007
www.gaiafriends.org/search.txt.html

After a millennia of separation and disjointedness, it is clearly time to work on healing ourselves, first and foremost, because only after having done so will we be able to assist in the healing of Mother Earth.

It has been the patriarchal culture and its model of dominance that has served to introduce the linked concepts of separation and duality; as a result, these traits have come to be further associated with the superior male and the secondary, or inferior, female.

In keeping with the Native American way, *it is now time for us as a planet to return to the unity and harmony, but to do it with full consciousness, with all that we have learned, to fully integrate both the masculine and the feminine.* [191]

I was most pleasantly surprised to discover some pertinent information that addresses the Prime Creator as a female vibration.

---

[191] Briar, Kathy. *In Search of The Feminine Divine.* Retrieved March 8, 2007
www.gaiafriends.org/search.txt.html

In truth, one should not find this premise to be a shocking one; after all, it is not the woman who has always given birth to new life on this planet.

Why, then, should it be any different with the Creator? It may, however, be shocking for men to think that perhaps a female vibration could be the source behind all things. [192]

I have always believed the trinity to encompass [1] Father God, [2] Mother God and [3] Son or Daughter of God; as a result, striking a male and female balance, even within one's self, is imperative to the creation of a peaceful world.

The *female* version of self encompasses intuition, receptivity, creativity, compassion and nourishment. The *male* version of self equates to powerful, rational and intellectual. What is now essential is the integration of the male and female essence, within yourself, for such makes you whole.

---

[192] Marciniak, Barbara. (1994). Earth: Pleiadian Keys to the Living Library (page90). Rochester, VT: Bear & Company Publishing.

In this regard, it becomes important to stay focused on your own growth, your own path, your own self.

It is equally important that one not concern themselves with what others are doing, as all are here to complete the same.

The Mother Goddess represents the love principle; hence, working with the Goddess energy requires a deeper exploration of this feminine principle.

If every woman took the time to explain to someone else what it is like to be a woman, what would they say?

Would they talk about what it means to give birth? Would they talk about what it means to love what they have created?

Might that love be protective or allowing?

One experiences true growth and evolving, as an individual, if they allow their children the freedom with which to experience their own selves as the magnificent beings that they are.

It goes without saying, however, that one has to limit freedom when it comes to very young children, gradually allowing them to come into their own.

In reference to the Garden of Eden, the female vibration was given the name Eve; however, she was not the first female. In the version that we have been introduced to, woman sprang from the rib of the man; namely, Adam.

As the maker of life, so, too, does the Goddess also bring forth life, for it is she who carries the blood; as a result, the story was changed to make it appear as if the male vibration had the ability to make life. [193]

The instructions of the Goddess are to *honor your bodies and Earth and your sexuality, because it is through this process that you are all created.* [194] No doubt, the midwife was considered to be the greatest enemy to the Christian religion because she could alleviate pain, she could tell other

[193] Marciniak, Barbara. (1994). Earth: Pleiadian Keys to the Living Library (pages 104 and 105). Rochester, VT: Bear & Company Publishing.
[194] Ibid, page 100.

women about the mysteries of their bodies, and she understood herbs. [195]

The primary work of the Goddess involves relationship. It is important that we develop relationships with each other (love partnerships, sexual partnerships, business, community and family) in an effect to better understand that we are all connected, male and female.

Many individuals, in their efforts to re-balance their feminine and masculine aspects, may look outside of themselves, seeking, and joining, a spirituality study group for support and enlightenment purposes. Some may decide to take up the ancient art of belly dancing, an art which began in the Middle East. Others, like myself, may prefer to re-explore Goddess spirituality through extensive reading.

Although the method of choice may be as different as there are individuals, in the end, all seek balance within themselves. *What must come to the forefront of the world's*

---

[195] Marciniak, Barbara. (1994). Earth: Pleiadian Keys to the Living Library (page 100). Rochester, VT: Bear & Company Publishing.

paradigm is an understanding of what life is, what death is, what all species are, and the fact that everything is interconnected; that everything is connected to the same source. [196]

As webmistress of <u>Portals of Spirit</u>, I was honored to meet Stéphane Wuttunee, a Plains Cree and French Canadian public speaker. We began email corresponding for several years, finally meeting, face to face, in April 2006, while he was attempting a cross-Canada trek for the environment.

As expressed in one of his letters, *beauty and harmony can be elusive creatures in today's world, and yet, amidst the social and environmental chaos, I see much order and hope. Dandelions continue to thrive even in the most inhospitable and polluted locations. The bull elk's haunting cry can still be heard echoing in the mountain breeze and the mighty eagle still rides the thermals. Many gifted individuals have also graced my path with their presence. These souls are*

---

[196] Marciniak, Barbara. (1994). <u>Earth: Pleiadian Keys to the Living Library</u> (page 91). Rochester, VT: Bear & Company Publishing.

dedicated to making this realm more like how it could be rather than more like what it has become. These people are enlightened spirits of the highest calibre and will not stop until their task is done; they are the Lightworkers.

In May 2006, I had hoped to finally meet another enlightened soul by the name of Joelle Houze.

Although Joelle and I had met online several years previous, both enrolled in a Spiritual Peacemaking course offered by James Twyman, the Peace Troubador, it was not meant to be.

Born in Strasbourg, France, Joelle worked as a Professor of Acupuncture for 3 ½ years at Yuin University in Los Angeles, California; so, too, has she worked at both the Griffith Observatory, as well as at NASA, serving on the board of International Society for Astrological Research (ISAR).

Given her work experiences, she has also given classes and talks on various subjects ranging from the Photon Belt to TCM (Traditional Chinese Medicine).

As well, Joelle has established healing centers (in both California and Wisconsin) based on light, love and energetic medicine.

In keeping with a Cathar prophecy ... **The Heart of the Dove is the journey of the Cathar and brings the return of the Laurel after 700 years** ... the aim of Joelle's journey was to activate the flight of the Dove.

She began her North American trek by activating one wing in both Vancouver as well as California. The other wing, due for activation, was situated across Newfoundland, the province where I live and work, as well as New York.

In the process of the journey, it was discovered that one wing had been injured; as a result, we used Laurel leaves to represent the continued voyage of the Holy Spirit (Dove) and its healing, with our prayers and ceremonial embrace.

As Joelle was not able to make it to Newfoundland, my friend Linda and I took it upon ourselves to have our own ceremony, burning laurel leaves that Joelle had sent from the Languedoc (the southern France area of the Cathars).

In Joelle's estimation, this was Spirit's way of assuring that no one person could lay claim to the work being done; purification and healing could now begin.

Upon leaving France, in May 2006, she returned to the Heart of the Dove where the Wildcat Medicine Wheel took place at Wildcat Mountain (near Viroqua, Wisconsin) on June 10th and 11th.

Linda had been able to gather some laurel leaves from her own property trees; these were sent to Joelle in Wisconsin, thereby linking Newfoundland with the celebration of dance, song, drumming and prayer for the healing of all transgressions in the North American continent, thereby giving love and light to Mother Earth, asking that this wildcat planet consciousness be transformed into the Heart of the Dove.

Joelle had also been told that the rise of the Golden Eagle would follow thereafter. In preparation for our Galactic Citizenship, Joelle was also been busy collecting signatures from people who were willing to walk for peace in a world without boundaries, to be presented at the UN office in New York City.

To have taken the journey as far as she has been led, and permitted, continues to be an incredible blessing.

There have been many who have been guided to bury crystals, to hold fires, to engage in both prayers as well as sweats.

We are only the outer manifestations of Spirit upon the face of the Earth; as such, Joelle has also been privy to a dream that has disclosed that by the spring of 2015, love on the planet will have reached critical mass. For this, she gives deep thanks.

The dawn of the Age of Aquarius is here; change is upon us, there is no stopping it. Love is both Lord and Lady of all life.

Although the words that now follow are not my own, I find that they are in keeping with the necessity we are now being faced with; namely, the re-balancing of ourselves.

It is the nature of man to seek happiness. Love is the wine of divine intoxication that fills the cup of our mortal lives with the happiness that we seek. It is the love we give to God and others that makes our lives full of meaning and pregnant with joy as each moment so lived gives birth to the splendor of the Infinite Reality. [197]

To find love, it will be necessary to cut away the knotted jungle of our own self-centered existence. This task is not for the faint of heart. However, it is the only way for us to truly love God and to love one another. Cutting away this jungle of deluded narcissistic self-absorption is what Jesus had in mind when he said: Do not suppose that I have come to bring peace to the earth. I did not come to bring peace, but a sword. Matthew 10:34, NIV [198]

----

[197] Walker III, Ethan. (2003). <u>The Mystic Christ: The Light of Non-Duality and the Path of Love According to the Life and Teachings of Jesus</u> (page 1). Norman, OK: Devi Press.
[198] Ibid, pages 1 and 2.

The "sword" in this case exists solely for the liberation of the soul that it may soar into the boundless sky of love. It is a sword of uncompromising compassion. [199]

During the period of the Inquisition tens of thousands were deprived of their property, banished or executed by burning at the stake because of their beliefs. This attitude still exists today, smoldering in the dark depths of our collective unconscious, constantly calling for its consort, ignorance, to unlock the gates of hell and unleash its fury. Bigotry, prejudice, intolerance and ethnic cleansing are but a few of its names. It was this attitude that Jesus challenged. [200]

It is my firm belief that the nature of humankind is good, but that we have clearly lost our way.

The more compassion we have for each other, the quicker mass consciousness will change.

---

[199] Walker III, Ethan. (2003). <u>The Mystic Christ: The Light of Non-Duality and the Path of Love According to the Life and Teachings of Jesus</u> (page 2). Norman, OK: Devi Press.
[200] Ibid.

It is essential that I love myself and Mother Earth; as well, there is a need to mentally let go of attachments while learning to reside in the peace and clarity of the moment.

Michele's Daily Affirmations

I have taken the words of Bob Proctor to create a new daily affirmation for myself.

I am living in an abundance of great health, increasing wealth and thriving relationships ... life is good.

As Sandy Gallagher puts it (courtesy of an email that I received).

It is easy to expect an undesirable outcome without even realizing it. The work lies in maintaining an awareness of your expectation and avoiding the habit of going on 'autopilot.' What is your habitual way of being? Think about this - are you naturally and automatically happy, upbeat and positive? Or is your tendency to have a more cautious and worrisome approach to life? The expectations you have and the way you respond have a direct effect on the results you are getting.

It is so very important that we continue to work to be cognizant of that which we expect.

Each must learn to be deliberate with their expectations.

I expect only the best.

———————————❖———————————

In the words of Albert Einstein … *I have considered myself to be very fortunate in that I have been able to do mostly only that which my inner self told me to do. I am also aware that I do receive much criticism from the outside world for what I do and some people actually get angry at me. But this does not really touch me because I feel that these people do not live in the same world as do I.*

I am here to live that which I know and understand to be my Truth.

I Am the Creator of My Life

Everything in the universe is made of energy; we often refer to this energy as vibration. Your thoughts and emotions are also energy-based; the combination of the two make up what is often referred to as your vibrational state.

The Law of Attraction resonates with your vibrations, so no matter what it is that you ask for, it is actually your vibrational state that serves to produce the outcome.

The key to making the Law of Attraction work for you is to *feel good* before you place your cosmic order.

Take the time to notice what you are grateful for; once you have raised your vibration in this manner, then take the time to place that order.

The final step lies in trusting the process; the step where you willingly let go, knowing that everything happens naturally and in its own perfect time.

The observer effect in quantum mechanics indicates that the quantum wave function collapses when an observation is made by an observer; in essence, the act of observing serves to influence the phenomenon being observed.

Under this same interpretation, this also means that there has had to have been an observer in place since the beginning of time.

Is not the observer, then, the creator of the universe?

Can it not be said, then, that this act of observing the universe is what served to bring it forth into being?

Therein lies the connection between the consciousness of the mind and the consciousness of the physical surroundings; the observer, then, plays a key role in how consciousness unfolds, and, as a result, you *create your own reality experience*.

To my way of thinking, everything that exists is, ultimately, God; there is nothing, then, that is not God.

Life itself is a mysterious and spectacular phenomenon; the beauty of this is limited only by how much of it you want to see.

If you want to know what divinity is, take the time to expand upon your inner knowingness.

———————————————————

According to Deepak Chopra, *God is the field of consciousness that creates, governs, and controls the manifest world. This consciousness has an invisible aspect beyond space and time. We can posit that there was no space or time before the Big Bang, yet there had to be something that allowed the universe and the laws of nature to coalesce with such amazing orderliness than with the slightest deviation, life could not have evolved.* [201]

---

[201]

www.beliefnet.com/columnists/intentchopra/2010/03/which-is-real-the-moon-or-god.html

In continuation, *consciousness, or God, also permeates creation once it appeared. We know this because we partake of consciousness, creativity, and intelligence. Where could we get those qualities if God, the source of consciousness, were gone?* [202]

At the core of existence, consciousness operates with no separation of observer, the observed, and the process of observation; the fallacy was in assuming that the observer could be erased from the picture. [203]

Not so, because consciousness both observes itself and it observes its creations; in effect, God does the same thing, which is why sages have wondered if everything doesn't take place in God's mind.[204]

Ultimately, of course, it does, but you have to adopt a new model of God that is consciousness.

202

www.beliefnet.com/columnists/intentchopra/2010/03/which-is-real-the-moon-or-god.html
[203] Ibid.
[204] Ibid.

There exists a mindful difference between how one responds and how one reacts. [205] [206] [207] [208]

It becomes imperative, then, that each learns to choose their response.

As one begins to expand their spiritual consciousness, they begin to realize that there is more to life, and the universe, than meets the eye, for creation is simply too astounding and phenomenal to be deemed haphazard; in truth, there is a oneness that pervades everything.

This energy, this essence, this life force, includes us, nature and the very universe itself; better yet, it has a consciousness.

---

[205] https://zenhabits.net/respond/

[206] https://www.huffingtonpost.com/lori-stevicrust-phd-abpp/react-respond_b_4252438.html

[207] https://www.psychologytoday.com/blog/making-change/201307/dont-just-react-choose-your-response

[208] https://tinybuddha.com/blog/respond-instead-of-reacting-speak-your-truth-not-your-fears/

As your spiritual consciousness grows even further, you also feel, and manifest, the real world spiritual values that are the reflections of unselfish loving (compassion, kindness, caring, giving, sharing and harmlessness) for these are the earmarks of true spirituality, taking us back to both Jesus and Buddha.

When such a spiritual change takes place within you, everyone you come into contact with will be better off having known you, for they, too, will have the ability to change in order to spread the beauty of unselfish love to others.

Like multiple ripples in a pond that are created from the throwing of just one rock, this unselfish love makes you a physical vehicle for the universal spirit, as it moves through you, and, thus, through the world.

———————————❈———————————

Jon Peniel has stated that *when you become enlightened, you are very, very busy helping others to attain the same freedom, peace, and unselfish love you have found, or you go on and ascend to a higher vibrational plane. If you stay, you work for the universal spirit, so to speak. You align your will, with universal will, and thus you become very busy doing your little part in the universal flow.* [209]

In keeping, *according to the teachings of the Atlantean Children of the Law of One, universal principles dictate that the kind of world you live in, and the creation of your future world, is all up to you. It is entirely your choice, and in your power to change, all by just making changes in yourself.* [210]

Quite clearly, he is speaking of the Law of Attraction, a universal reality which means, quite simply, that we attract into our lives that which we focus on and give power (energy) to, whether it be negative (fear, anger, worry, stress, hate) or positive (love, peace of mind, health, well-being, wealth, success, happiness).

---

[209] Peniel, Jon. (1997). The Children of the Law of One and The Lost Teachings of Atlantis (page 37). Alamosa, CO: Network.
[210] Ibid, pages 41-42.

You can fully expect that there will be many trials and tribulations as you change inside to become a better person, but ultimately it will be done, if it is your will to do so.

The world outside of the physical you will change according to the changes you make within yourself. Buddha understood this universal law when he stated that *we are shaped by our thoughts,* thereby becoming what we think.

Regardless of whether or not you believe it, your beliefs control your destiny. Whatever we do, we do to ourselves.

There is a law of karma that says one reaps what one sows, be it by way of thoughts, feelings, intentions or actions. This, in and of itself, should offer compelling spiritual reflection, most imperative for self-examination, given that we are the creators of our own misery.

Beliefs have a dominant and powerful effect on every aspect of one's life. We know that there exist individuals willing to kill over their beliefs; it is for this important reason that each of us needs to closely scrutinize the beliefs that we hold, because of what they create in our lives.

→Do your beliefs further the manifestations of unselfish love or do they inhibit the manifestations of unselfish love?

→Do your beliefs breed anger, hatred and harm or do they breed tranquility, love and healing?

→Do your beliefs make for a better life or do they make for a worse life?

→Do your beliefs make for a better world for others or do they make for a worse world for all of us?

We live in a world that has created the illusion of separateness from the universal spirit; this illusion has served as the basis for creating selfishness. *Those who know not that they are one, act not as one. Those who act not as one, create not love, but suffering and disharmony. What you create, you receive.* [211] In essence, the fruits of your acts will continue to follow you all of your days.

---

[211] Peniel, Jon. (1997). <u>The Children of the Law of One and The Lost Teachings of Atlantis</u> (page 63). Alamosa, CO: Network.

When we talk about the state of a person's consciousness, *we are essentially talking about the state of their awareness of the world around them. And as such, a person's consciousness is directly related to the way they view, interpret, understand, and interact with, everyone and everything around them.* [212]

A person's point of view is affected by *both the state of their consciousness, and their beliefs and programming. Beliefs and programming are usually in sync with a person's level of consciousness. However, consciousness is dominant, and if there is a shift to a higher or lower state, the new consciousness can alter and override a person's beliefs and programming in order to match the new level of consciousness.* [213]

We are here to regain consciousness of our Oneness with everything.

---

[212] Peniel, Jon. (1997). <u>The Children of the Law of One and The Lost Teachings of Atlantis</u> (page 65). Alamosa, CO: Network.
[213] Ibid.

This can only be attained through unselfish love, looking to both Jesus and Buddha as important and living examples; we must see the illusions of self consciousness that we carry with us in our mind and break them.

God is Love. Give Love and You Give God. Give Love and You Get God. [214]

If Your Thoughts Are Not Accompanied By Feeling Unselfish Love, Can What You Are Thinking Be Correct? [215]

Find Oneness at All Cost. In finding Oneness, you find God. In finding Oneness, you find yourself. In finding Oneness, you find Real Love. Living as One, is to Unselfishly Love All. Living as One, is to Unselfishly Love yourself. To find Oneness, Unselfishly Love others before yourself. [216]

---

[214] Peniel, Jon. (1997). <u>The Children of the Law of One and The Lost Teachings of Atlantis</u> (page 93). Alamosa, CO: Network.
[215] Ibid, page 94.
[216] Ibid, page 93.

In continuing to strive forward on a spiritual, metaphysical, and, somewhat, philosophical journey, I am feeling more and more liberated from the yoke of repression, a yoke which continues to exist in an attempt to keep all enslaved through power and control (courtesy of fear and guilt).

In keeping with my own personal affirmation, **I am the co-creator of my life, working in sync with the enlightening, intelligent and energetic universe**, each time I continue to say these words aloud with *intense* feeling, I am succeeding in becoming more and more empowered.

I feel a deep sense of overwhelming gratitude at being able to stand tall (all five feet of me), verbalize and feel the authority of these very words.

Everyone lives in the world of his or her thoughts. Thoughts are energy; hence, positive thoughts attract positive results, naturally, while negative thoughts attract negative results.

Our thoughts, beliefs, expectations, words and actions create a magnetic field around us that attracts to us people and situations that match our energy and our vibration.

In this regard, know what you want; monitor your thoughts carefully, being sure to only think about what you want, because the universe will take a snapshot of your thoughts for manifestation purposes.

What shows up in your life has <u>less</u> to do with where you were born and how you were raised and <u>more</u> to do with what you <u>think about</u>, what you <u>focus on</u>, what you <u>talk about</u>, what you <u>act upon</u> and what <u>you believe</u>.

Everything is the result of mere thought; this being so, it is *the mind that is the builder* towards a caring, unselfish and harmless world.

———————✻———————

Gratitude for every aspect of your life, including what is yet to come, is key; too often, in our busy lives, we forget to be grateful for what we have.

Take the time to stop and appreciate the good in your life.

Take the time to stop and appreciate the positive in your life.

Take the time to stop and appreciate the uplifting in your life.

Be thankful for your health.

Be thankful for life.

Be thankful for your achievements.

Be thankful for nature.

Be thankful for everyone and everything that contributes to this magnificent and miraculous journey.

As you become truly appreciative for everything in your life, including those things yet to arrive, you will be truly amazed at how much the feeling of gratitude opens the floodgates of the universe to bring everything to you.

In addition, it is of the utmost importance that we take the time to live more authentically as per Robert Rabbin: [217]

[1] Live your own life in both strength and courage as opposed to living the life that someone else wants, or expects, you to live.

[2] Be persistent as you continue to build your dream, whatever it may be. Be persistent, but also flexible because flexibility allows us to learn from our mistakes, and to learn from others, embracing change when necessary.

[3] Respect other people, especially those that you do not like or who are so completely different from you that you appear to have no common ground. Respecting other people invites them to respect you. If you do no harm to others, and they, in turn, respond in kind, one can only imagine the beauty of this planet.

---

[217] https://www.stillnessspeaks.com/teacher/robert-rabbin/

[4] Express gratitude and appreciation to everyone, each and every day; it takes but a moment, and yet it makes all the difference in the world. This is the formula for creating Heaven on earth.

[5] Live in the moment because now is the only time there is. Make it count; strive to be your very best in each moment. Be not afraid to face your fears. Be not afraid to speak the truth of who you are, taking the time to live from the depths of your soul.

[6] Knowing that we all face an uncertain future, do not allow yourself to become cynical and selfish; we can face this future together. Whilst it may seem that we cannot change things, we must continue to stand up for righteousness and justice for all. Remember to take care of yourself and your families, but continue to make a contribution to others. Find a way to be of service to the world. Find a way to be of service to others. Keep a positive outlook and remain optimistic at all times.

A Personal Connection

The Goddess represents the divine feminine; the God represents the divine masculine.

On a manifested level, this translates to a physical woman and a physical man; regardless of whether we are male or female, we all have divine feminine and divine masculine energy within us.

In keeping, we all share a connection with Sophia, the feminine aspect of the Divine Logos, the Wisdom of God, the Holy Spirit; so, too, has she also been compared to the divine spark that resides within all of us.

Not only does she represent Wisdom, but she is also denoted as the Bride of Christ; in truth, her story is our story ... the soul's adventure across infinity wherein she waits for us to recognize her as both the manifest mind of God as well as the manifest mind of God in every person we meet whilst on this sojourn.

That having been said, Mary Magdalene can be symbolized further as Sophia (Wisdom), the Holy Spirit, and the triple Goddess (the original Holy Trinity).

It is in the coming together of divine feminine and divine masculine, the two energies, that we become balanced, that we become One.

It is in the merging of the ego (mind) with the heart (wisdom) that creates a new way of thinking; hence, when the inner (heart, wisdom, soul) and the outer (mind) are joined together in love, you have entered the kingdom.

Not just the name of an individual, Magdalene is also the name of an order of consciousness that is re-emerging.

All are here to embrace their own inner Magdalene; in so doing, it is equally important to realize that each chooses the reality in which he (she) dwells.

For most of us, our realities shift and change based on thoughts, beliefs, words and actions; whenever one of these variables changes, so does the reality that is experienced.

Our *real* power is to be found within the heart. In keeping, we have begun to come full circle in understanding what the ancients knew about the heart, the brain, and divine consciousness. [218] [219] [220] [221]

The heart generates the largest electromagnetic field in the body; a field that is 60 times greater in amplitude than brain waves. Research continues to show that a person's emotional state is communicated via signals sent to the brain by the heart neurons; hence, keeping yourself in alignment with what your heart loves enables you to stay happy and healthy.

The electromagnetic signals produced by your heart are also registered in the brain waves of the people around you; in this way, we affect everyone.

---

[218] https://www.youtube.com/watch?v=7c3AVj66ahg
[219] thespiritscience.net
[220] www.social-consciousness.com/2012/09/awakening-the-illuminated-healing-heart-power.html
[221] https://justinahurley.wordpress.com/2012/05/05/10-things-to-know-about-the-power-of-the-heart/

There is a fascinating monograph, <u>The Energetic Heart: Bioelectromagnetic Interactions Within and Between People</u>, written by Rollin McCraty, Ph.D., [222] [223] that shows *when people touch, or are in proximity, a transference of the electromagnetic energy produced by the heart occurs.* This energy transference, be it positive or negative, is based on the emotional state of the person transmitting the emotions; hence, everything you do matters, everything you think matters, everything you feel matters, everything you enact upon matters.

Doing what we love, being around loving people, and treating others with love and respect, is not just something we need to think about and reflect upon; it is something we must emanate outward into the world. Following your heart (your inner desires, your passion, what makes you feel alive) is critical to your heart's health and well-being; it becomes in the sustaining of positive emotions that you are able to generate increased heart rhythm coherence.

---

[222] store.heartmath.org/e-books/energetic-heart.html
[223] https://www.heartmath.org/research/

Jesus (Greek) Joshua (Hebrew) is the personification of the creative spirit of every human being. [224]

Mary, as bride, is the feminine aspect of the Christ, and her inner marriage, is to be an enlightened human being. [225]

As a spiritually conscious human being, operating solely from a heart based consciousness, you will find that you can no longer be used, or manipulated, by your own ego (or the unconscious egocentric people around you); this becomes the time when you are able to help others find this same ability in themselves.

As an awakened human being *you are aware of the world of forms in which you move; at the same time, there is increased awareness of the formless creative presence out of which all form continually emerges, and into which it continually dissolves*; this is what the Greek texts of the gospels call the Christos. [226]

---

[224] https://patternsofcreation.com/tag/sophia/
[225] Ibid.
[226] Ibid.

The more present we are in each moment, the more we will begin to create as Living Masters of the physical and metaphysical (spiritual) realms.

What is the Holy Grail?

I see the Holy Grail as an alchemical marriage of sorts; a spiritual alchemical marriage of heaven and earth.

Based on everything that I have come to understand in my own journey, thus far, the point is *to know the Grail, not as a cup, but as a process*; a process through which our purpose is of a two-fold nature, meaning that [1] we can either "transcend matter; perpetually renouncing anything connected with the principle of power, and, thereby, attaining union with the principle of love," [227] or [2] we can "reclaim or redeem matter, spiritualizing and transforming it." [228]

In reference to physical beings, lead is the base material, meaning "negative thoughts, lustful passions and harmful emotions, which the aspirant of alchemy must change, or transmute, into the spiritual or gold; lead represents the

---

[227] www.serenitytravels.com/cathar_missions.html
[228] Ibid.

chaotic, heavy and sick condition of metal or the inward man [whereas] gold expresses the perfection of both metallic and human existence," [229] of which pure love is key.

Alchemy also teaches "the raising of vibrations: the belief in the ability to transmute or change matter to a higher level. One of the most important principles that the alchemists used has to do with the basic duality of the universe. The method of procedure to achieve the Philosopher's Stone is [none other than] the harmonizing of this duality." [230]

As such, alchemists believe that everything, including man, can be raised to a higher level of being. This is what is meant by the term *illumination*; a term that also references death of the earthly self. In order to progress on the spiritual path, one must die to the old way of life (the ego, the illusions, the extravagances). It is not to say, however, that we cannot enjoy physical possessions; the problem lies in the significance that they are given.

---

[229] *Alchemy from the Spiritual Venturer* website accessed on April 2, 2012 at www.denverspiritualcommunity.org/Wisdom/Alchemy.htm
[230] Ibid.

As we turn inward, through meditation or contemplative prayer, so, too, do we, once again, *become as little children*, in that we are able to reconnect with our true spiritual selves. This heightened (elevated) consciousness enables us to combine body, mind and soul in a new way; a most powerful force for transformation.

———————————————

Alchemists were sometimes known as the Fire Philosophers.

From an allegorical point of view, they "sought to consume themselves in spiritual flames in order to find their true, pure, essential selves. The furnace was the human body, where hardened thoughts and emotions (metals) were to be heated in the hermetically sealed vessel of the mind until purified." [231]

---

[231] *Alchemy from the Spiritual Venturer* website accessed on April 2, 2012 at www.denverspiritualcommunity.org/Wisdom/Alchemy.htm

Every time we are successful in disengaging from the ego (meaning the material and transitory existence), we find ourselves advancing closer to the spiritual values that bring true happiness and fulfillment. While this can be a painful process, so, too, is it a necessary one.

All must begin with the perfected feminine (meaning the heart) that "brings us to a most elevated state of the emotions: a peace and joy which is above the opposition of the duality of the natural." [232] Part of this process involves eliminating negative emotions from your life; such is accomplished by replacing them with positive ones (thereby leading to the actual transmutation process). As one learns to spiritualize the mind in this way, a process that involves transmuting the intellect (the masculine component) so that the ego becomes willing to give up control to the developing Soul, the newly evolving spiritual consciousness, one must guard against becoming depressed.

---

[232] *Alchemy from the Spiritual Venturer* website accessed on April 2, 2012 at www.denverspiritualcommunity.org/Wisdom/Alchemy.htm

A difficult and painful process, so, too, is it a process through which "the insight gained from the elevation of the emotions enables us to realize our inherent deficiencies." [233]

It is this very lengthy (slow) and diligent process that is often referenced as the *dark night of the soul*; a process that is instrumental to the awakening of consciousness.

Eventually one arrives at the enhanced knowledge that in order to continue their spiritual growth, they must learn to stand their ground, maintaining their new belief set in the full, knowing that they are responsible only for themselves.

This becomes the very beginning of conscious spirit residing within the physical body, an awakening that leads to the realization that "to become immortal, we must embrace our mortality, [and] to become truly spiritual beings, we must accept ourselves as we are, and also as we are becoming,"

---

[233] *Alchemy from the Spiritual Venturer* website accessed on April 2, 2012 at
www.denverspiritualcommunity.org/Wisdom/Alchemy.htm

[234] for therein lies the truth behind the alchemical marriage between the enlightened heart and the illumined mind; the result of which is, none other than, the Philosopher's Stone.

As the clear mind (uninhibited by the ego) joins with the heart, one's spiritual essence (one's purity of heart) shines forth most strongly, for this is "true integration, true wholeness; the sacred marriage of the mind or consciousness with the heart or unconsciousness in one totally conscious being. At this point of conjunction, all opposition has been overcome." [235]

It must be remembered, however, that in learning to accomplish this wholeness, one has had to learn to embrace, and accept, their inherent weaknesses.

---

[234] *Alchemy from the Spiritual Venturer* website accessed on April 2, 2012 at www.denverspiritualcommunity.org/Wisdom/Alchemy.htm
[235] Ibid.

Let us now discuss *the squaring of the circle*, a motto that reads ... *Make a circle out of a man and woman, derive from it a square, and from the square a triangle: make a circle and you will have the Philosopher's Stone.* [236]

It is the inner circle around the man and the woman that symbolizes the Chemical Marriage of the Mind and the Heart whist the square around this smaller circle represents the four elements; none other than fire, earth, air and water; all of which are incorporated in the process. [237]

The square, being four sided, also signifies the number 4, which reflects wholeness, the four directions, and so forth. [238]

With the triangle surrounding the square indicating the union of the body, soul and spirit, along with the implication of the result of this union, it is the apex, or the third point

---

[236] *Alchemy from the Spiritual Venturer* website accessed on April 2, 2012 at
www.denverspiritualcommunity.org/Wisdom/Alchemy.htm
[237] Ibid.
[238] Ibid.

above, which further indicates the spiritual perfection that has, thusly, been achieved. [239]

http://mormonmatters.org/2010/01/29/squaring-the-circle-balance-and-ideals/

---

[239] *Alchemy from the Spiritual Venturer* website accessed on April 2, 2012 at www.denverspiritualcommunity.org/Wisdom/Alchemy.htm

The circle, thereby enclosing the whole diagram, represents a transformation of the body, mind and soul, one so complete that the man becomes the woman and the woman becomes the man; the two truly become one. [240]

In truth, *without the man* (or mind) *and the woman* (or heart), there would be no Christ Consciousness or Illumination. [241]

The most important result of this marriage (of heart and mind) is the subsequent birth of the soul, the Christ; this is what alchemists sometimes called *the child of the Work*, meaning that this was the beginning of the building of an actual second body, the spiritual body wherein the Christ consciousness (the path to our own soul illumination) would dwell. [242]

------

[240] *Alchemy from the Spiritual Venturer* website accessed on April 2, 2012 at
www.denverspiritualcommunity.org/Wisdom/Alchemy.htm
[241] Ibid.
[242] Ibid.

In the words of Dr. R. Swinburne Clymer ... "The extraordinary or spiritualized threefold man is the outgrowth of the four-square-man. After the ordinary man has awakened to a sense of something higher than life, as we daily see it, and has sought for, and found, the means to the greater life, if truly interested he will then take active steps to develop every department of his fourfold nature." [243]

This means that "he will seek to learn just what the body requires, what it should be given and what should be withheld. He will endeavor, by every means in his power, to bring his body into as perfect a state as possible and make use of as much spirit as is necessary and become *spiritually alive*; that is to say, full of vitality, magnetism, virility or whatever we wish to name his life-full state." [244]

---

[243] *Alchemy from the Spiritual Venturer* website accessed on April 2, 2012 at
www.denverspiritualcommunity.org/Wisdom/Alchemy.htm
[244] Ibid.

By gradual degrees, "he applies the mind to the development of the germ of the Immortal Soul within himself. He becomes the Builder. The Soul Spark is awakened and eventually becomes Illuminated. The Soul takes the place of the mind and man completes the circle. He has reversed the squaring of the circle and once again becomes a threefold being; a circle symbolized by the triangle." [245]

In keeping with this process, there are many lessons to be learned, there is much knowledge to be sought, and there is much wisdom to be attained and applied. In direct association, it must be acknowledged that the working through of these highlighted lessons is a due process that spans many years, requiring much diligence.

<hr />

In words that have been attributed to Appollonius of Tyana, *Be ye renewed through the renewing of your mind.*

---

[245] *Alchemy from the Spiritual Venturer* website accessed on April 2, 2012 at www.denverspiritualcommunity.org/Wisdom/Alchemy.htm

Religion versus Spirituality

One can easily define being religious as being associated with an established religious institution.

Being spiritual, on the other hand, is a more nebulous term; generally speaking, it can mean feeling drawn to, or associated with, something metaphysical (mystical, esoteric, philosophical) without needing to be a member of a group.

On a deeper level, one can distinguish between types of religion and spirituality as being either exoteric or esoteric.

The exoteric is the outer or conventional level that consists of belief systems, doctrines, ceremonies and institutions whereby one believes certain things and behaves in a specific fashion. The deeper, often hidden, esoteric level is all about specific practices that transform the practitioner; so, too, can this include the community of those who engage these transformative practices, as well as the guiding teacher who instructs, and initiates, these practitioners.

It is possible to be religious without being spiritual and spiritual without being religious.

Based on the definitions shared herein, *belief* versus *being* (practice) appears to be the line that divides the two.

Many believers of religion argue for the importance of believing in God, asserting that God has instructed humanity to behave in certain ways, and not others; they may also claim that it is their duty to persuade (and sometimes coerce) others into following those instructions. [246]

By comparison, esoteric spiritual practitioners often say that what you believe is much less important than what you do, especially what you do with your attention. [247]

We know there to be practices that engage both the body and the mind (such as meditation and yoga).

---

[246] https://io9.com/what-will-religion-be-like-in-the-future-1524424632
[247] Ibid.

When people practice these disciplines of attention correctly, they often experience greater mental clarity and less emotional reactivity; if you go deeper, you may also experience extraordinary states of consciousness.

True spirituality (your way of loving, your way of accepting, your way of relating to the world and the people around you) is something that is found deep within; it cannot be found in a church or by believing in a certain way.

The earmarks of true spirituality encompass caring, kindness, compassion, giving and harmlessness; the very virtues associated with both Buddha and Yeshua.

Religion versus Spirituality [248] [249]

---

[248] https://www.bibliotecapleyades.net/mistic/mistic_10.htm
[249]
https://www.biographyonline.net/spiritual/articles/religion_vs_spirituality.html

Esoteric Spirituality

The word esoteric comes from the Greek work *esoterikos* meaning inner or from within.

Jesus taught that the soul can expand the boundaries of everyday consciousness and experience higher levels of awareness all the way to cosmic consciousness; this is what is known as esoteric spirituality. In essence, then, esoteric spirituality is meant for the inner spiritual development of the soul.

The Ancient Greek aphorism *know thyself* is one of the Delphic maxims and was inscribed in the pronaos (forecourt) of the Temple of Apollo at Delphi; so, too, is this our ancient quest for self-knowledge. I personally equate *know thyself* with esoteric knowledge. Going within is the only way to understand that which is truth; in this manner, the physical body is the teacher, via thoughts, feelings, words, actions, emotions, the chakras, the energy bodies that surround the physical body, and the third eye.

In words belonging to Rumi ......*Moonlight floods the whole sky from horizon to horizon; how much it can fill your room depends on its windows.*

As shared by the 14th Dalai Lama ......*People take different roads seeking fulfillment and happiness. Just because they are not on your road does not mean they are lost.*

As written by Rudolph Steiner, in <u>Christianity as Mystical Fact</u> ...... *Let a divine being approach you! It may be nothing or everything. Nothing, if you meet it in the frame of mind in which you confront everyday things. Everything, if you are prepared and attuned to it. What it is in itself is a matter which does not concern you; the point is whether it leaves you as you were or makes a different man of you. But this depends solely on you. You must have been prepared by the education and development of the most intimate forces of your personality so that what the divine is able to evoke may be kindled and released in you. What is brought to you depends upon the reception you prepare for it.*

<u>A Course in Miracles</u> [250] [251] [252]

Awakened Blog [253]

Blavatsky Theosophy Group UK [254]

Discover Gnosis [255]

Emergent Light [256]

Esoteric and Spiritual Journals [257]

Esoteric Mystery School [258]

Esoteric Science [259]

---

[250] stobblehouse.com/text/ACIM.pdf
[251] courseinmiracles.com
[252] https://acim.org/Digital_Editions/kindle_ebook.html
[253] awakened1.blogspot.com
[254] https://blavatskytheosophy.com
[255] https://gnosticteachings.org
[256] meader.org
[257] www.servicegrowth.net/index.php?cat=31
[258] northernway.org/school.html
[259] https://www.esotericscience.org

Esoteric Science and Philosophy [260]

Fundamentals of the Esoteric Philosophy [261]

Hermetic Fellowship [262]

Hermetic Philosophy and the Mystery of Being [263]

House of the Sun [264]

Kheper [265]

Online Esoteric Library [266]

Simply Love [267]

The Basic Premises of Esoteric Spiritual Philosophy [268]

---

[260] https://edgeba.webs.com
[261] https://www.theosociety.org/pasadena/fund/fund-1.htm
[262] www.hermeticfellowship.org
[263] www.plotinus.com
[264] www.soul-guidance.com/houseofthesun/
[265] www.kheper.net/index.htm
[266] www.hermetics.org/ebooks.html
[267] https://integrallife.com/integral-post/simply-love
[268] www.attarmusic.com/page16/page20/page20.html

The Esoteric Tradition of Eastern Orthodoxy [269]

The Journey Through Life Series [270]

The Last Esoteric Message [271]

Theosophy Online [272]

The Hermetic Library [273]

The Soul Journey Blog [274]

Trans4Mind: Esoteric History and Philosophy [275]

Western Esoteric and Occult Texts [276]

269

https://www.bibliotecapleyades.net/esp_autor_mouravieff.ht
m

[270] soul-books.com/index.shtml

[271] www.gurdjiefflegacy.org/70links/esoteric.htm

[272] www.theosophyonline.com

[273] https://hermetic.com

[274] thesouljourney.com/blog/

[275] https://www.trans4mind.com/personal-development-
videos/videos-esoteric.html

[276] www.sacred-texts.com/eso/

Will the Esoteric Jesus Please Stand Up? [277]

World Spiritual Traditions: Theosophical Perspectives [278]

_____

[277] www.spiritofthescripture.com/id1442-will-the-esoteric-jesus-please-stand-up.html
[278]

www.theosophy-nw.org/theosnw/world/general/rel-selc.htm

As Above, So Below

Recorded in Hermetic texts, it has been stated that these words originated in the <u>Vedas</u> (the oldest layer of Sanskrit literature and the oldest scriptures of Hinduism).

The actual text of this maxim (a thought, a truth, an underlying principle, that can motivate individuals), as translated by Dennis W. Hauck from <u>The Emerald Tablet of Hermes Trismegistus</u>, is: *That which is Below corresponds to that which is Above, and that which is Above corresponds to that which is Below, to accomplish the miracle of the One Thing,* meaning that whatever happens on any level of reality (physical, emotional, mental, spiritual) also happens on every other level.

This means that what happens on the visible plane (what you can see right in front of your nose) also occurs on the invisible plane (spiritual places of the unseen realm) and vice versa; the material world is always an expression of the spiritual world.

This principle is often used to describe the microcosm and the macrocosm, with the microcosm being the self and the macrocosm being the universe.

In this manner, the macrocosm is as the microcosm and vice versa; within each lies the other, and through understanding one (usually the microcosm), man may begin to understand the other.

So, too, can it be said that the movement of the planets and the position of the stars, in the heavens, reflect available energies that we can either use or ignore.

As we attempt to understand ourselves, we also begin to understand the universe around us. It becomes imperative, then, that we

[1] take the time to look within and feel our power

[2] take the time to look within and remember our power

[3] take the time to look within and become our own perfected version of this same power (meaning God)

As above, so below, as within, so without, as the universe, so the soul…

Hermes Trismegistus

A Hyper-History of the Emerald Tablet [279]

Alchemy Study Program [280]

As Above, So Below [281] [282]

As Above, So Below Part 1 [283]

---

[279] https://www.alchemylab.com/hyper_history.htm
[280] www.alchemystudy.com/
[281]
https://www.themystica.com/mystica/articles/a/below_above.html
[282] www.abovetopsecret.com/forum/thread908599/pg1
[283] www.blavatsky.net/index.php/61-foundation/tf-newsletters/reed-carson-newsletters/449-as-above-so-below-part-i

As Above, So Below Part 2 [284]

Origin of As Above, So Below [285]

Tabula Smaragdina, the Emerald Table [286]

The Cosmic Wisdom of the Ancients [287]

The Emerald Tablet of Hermes [288]

The Emerald Tablet of Hermes: The Wisdom and Responsibility of the Rosicrucians [289]

---

[284] www.blavatsky.net/index.php/61-foundation/tf-newsletters/reed-carson-newsletters/450-as-above-so-below-part-ii
[285] https://radiantwoman.wordpress.com/2006/12/25/origin-of-as-above-so-below/
[286] www.sofiatopia.org/equiaeon/emerald.htm
[287] www.thelivingmoon.com/44cosmic_wisdom/menu.html
[288] www.sacred-texts.com/alc/emerald.htm
[289]

www.academia.edu/29702970/The_Emerald_Tablet_of_Hermes_The_Wisdom_and_Responsibility_of_the_Rosicrucians

The Emerald Tablets of Thoth the Atlantean [290] [291] [292]

The Kybalion of Hermes Trismegistus (full audio book) [293]

The Stone of the Philosophers: An Alchemical Handbook [294]

The World Within and the World Without [295]

---

[290]

www.horuscentre.org/library/Hermetism/The_Emerald_Tabl
ets_Of_Thoth.pdf
[291] https://www.bibliotecapleyades.net/thot/esp_thot_1.htm
[292] https://beforeitsnews.com/v3/watercooler-
topics/2013/2433444.html
[293] https://www.youtube.com/watch?v=UvV8vLON-nY
[294]

https://thehiddenoness.weebly.com/uploads/1/3/6/2/1362913
7/the_stone_of_the_philosophers.pdf
[295] www.mindreality.com/world-within-and-world-without

Our Sacred Connections

The Divine life force that inhabits our physical body is one with the Divine life force that created All That Is; hence, we are always connected to each other through a magnificent and eternal thread of invisible energy.

Throughout our search we reconnect and find the One, so, too, must we become the One; it is like Mahatma Gandhi has always stated, *we must become that which we seek.*

This means that everything starts with me.

My thoughts, my words, my actions; these are the very manifestation of the same Divine life force that I attract to myself.

This life force can be positive or negative, depending on what I think, I say, or I do.

Knowing that my outer world is a reflection of my inner world, there is one thing that I can always control: my thoughts.

A New Vision of Reality

A human being is part of the whole called by us universe, a part limited in time and space. He experiences himself, his thoughts and feelings as something separated from the rest, a kind of optical delusion of his consciousness. This delusion is a kind of prison for us, restricting us to our personal desires and to affection for a few persons nearest to us. Our task must be to free ourselves from this prison by widening our circle of compassion to embrace all living creatures and the whole of nature in its beauty.

Albert Einstein

Life is a Celebration

At the end of our days on this earth, after all our successes and failures, the measure of worth for our life will be how much we have loved.

Ammachi

If you think positively, Sound becomes Music, Movement Becomes Dance, Smile Becomes Laughter, Mind Becomes Meditation and Life Becomes a Celebration.

It is difficult to think positively in challenging situations and times but there is one little secret can be of help during these times. Pause before reacting; that is the Power of response. Once you take a pause, you bring the subconscious mind into play. You will be amazed to see your own positivity when you start practicing this simple but incredibly powerful technique.

Rishika Jain

Personal Meditations

The Shape of the Elements

Wiccan Morning Prayer

O Gracious Goddess,

O Gracious God,

Lend me health, strength and love

During this coming day.

Assist me with the challenges ahead.

Share Your divine wisdom.

Teach me to respect all things.

Remind me that the greatest power of all is love.

Blessed Be.

Wiccan Evening Prayer

Lady of the Moon,

Lord of the Sun.

Protect me and mine,

Now day is done.

http://wiccanmoonsongquotes.blogspot.ca/2012/02/daily-
spiritual-quote-february-7-2012.html

Universal Prayer   Shri Naath Devi

May all religions find a common ground of unity.

May all beings be happy.

May the poor be fed.

May the naked be clothed.

May the thirsty receive the waters of pure light.

May the deaf hear.

May the warmongers find refuge in peace.

May all beings love one another.

May all children be protected.

May all beings find simplicity.

May all beings realize their true nature.

May all races come together in brotherhood.

May the blind see.

May the lame walk.

May all beings that are lost find their way.

May all beings that are miserable surrender to truth.

May all beings that are sad find happiness.

May all beings that are unconscious be awakened.

May all beings that are lonely find the perfect companion.

May all beings that are mute be able to speak.

May all beings that are uneducated receive knowledge.

May all beings that are weak find strength.

May all beings that are brave be rewarded.

May all beings be happy.

May all beings be enlightened.

May peace prevail in all hearts.

May peace prevail on Earth.

Novus Spiritus Prayer

Dearest Heavenly Father and Heavenly Mother,

I humbly embrace the male and female aspects of my very essence; the male representing pure intellect and the female representing pure emotion.

Please guide me in the complete and integral integration of these two facets of my spiritual being.

Please guide me as a Divine instrument in the bringing about of Heaven on Earth.

Make me an instrument of your peace.

Amen

Fairy Ouroboros

Copyright © Rosie Lauren Smith [296]

The Ouroboros, a serpent in the form of a circle (Ananta-sesha) biting its tail, stands for eternity and boundless wisdom.

---

[296] fairytalenewsblog.blogspot.ca/2012/01/illustrations-by-rosie-lauren-smith.html

Today's Positive Thought

The time you take to experience your connection to the Divine is your most valuable investment.

Today's Positive Affirmation

I easily remember to stop and experience the Divine within several times today.

Today's Positive Visualization

As I take in a slow and even breath, my heart opens and a connection is easily made to the Divine spirit within me. I feel a loving, healing and warm presence flowing into my mind, my emotions and my body. In my mind's eye I see and feel this energy filling every cell of my being. I know that this Divine light is flowing into my life creating perfection everywhere it goes. I imagine the positive changes in my life as I allow the spirit presence to easily and continuously flow through me. I give thanks for this time of experiencing the Divine and send my light into the world. I combine these images with the feelings of joy and let them go, knowing that they will create the good things I am visualizing and thinking.

© Creative Living Foundation, INC

Michele's Insights

Courtesy of this work, the reader now knows that my parents, both raised within the Roman Catholic tradition, had their marriage annulled.

The RCC does not permit divorce, teaching that marriage is a lifelong commitment that cannot be dissolved through divorce; one can, however, have their marriage annulled.

In legal terminology, an annulment declares a marriage null and void; unlike divorce, an annulment is usually retroactive, meaning that an annulled marriage is considered to be invalid from the beginning (almost as if it had never taken place).

If one were to seek out a divorce without having procured an annulment, one could possibly run the risk of being ex-communicated from the church.

My parents were legally divorced when I was fifteen years of age.

To say that an invalid marriage can be dissolved, almost as if it had never taken place, was something that angered me, that distressed me, that challenged me.

All of a sudden, I felt as if I had been born on the wrong side of the blanket, a saying that references the fact that one is born of parents not lawfully married to each other.

Suffice it to say that this has, in the past, been deemed scandalous; an act wherein the blame is often leveled against the female for having lured the male into a perceived offense against the laws of morality. Unfortunately, so, too, do the children pay a price.

Did the church deem me illegitimate?

Would I now be referenced as a bastard?

It seemed clear, in my mind: while I was a child that could no longer be legitimated, I was still viewed as a soul that could be saved.

First, however, let me take you back in time so that you can better understand my earlier feelings towards the RCC.

As the oldest of five daughters, for too many years I felt quite alone; an outsider, it often felt as if I did not belong in my own physical body. Often, I would retreat into the world of my imagination, a world of colors, sights and smells; perhaps this is why I thoroughly enjoyed attending Mass as a child.

It would be years later, when I was well into my thirties, that I came to discover Moldavite, a tektite formed 15 million years ago during the impact of a giant meteorite. It was this very stone-like substance that served to assist me in feeling comfortable in this human body.

At the tender age of six years, I can still remember walking up the aisle to kneel and receive the Eucharist for the first time. Mesmerized by the rituals, smells (incense and candles), stained glass windows and statues, as a young lady in Grade 9, at the age of fourteen years, I was strongly gravitating towards a life career choice as a Nun within the RCC.

I always felt as if there were many that did not enjoy reciting the rosary. For me, this was a most profound experience in that I was able to *feel the words* with a sense of depth, love and compassion; so, too, was it the same for the recitation of sacred prayers that others seemed to rush through with careless abandon.

All of this changed after my parents were legally divorced.

I began to challenge the position of the church.

I could never understand why priests were not allowed to marry.

It made no sense to be counseled by the family priest, who was quick to offer advice on marriage, having children and raising a family, when he was both unwed and childless.

I can remember feeling much elation at learning, in my teenage years, that my former Grade 1 teacher had left the convent to marry a former priest from our parish.

Being an avid reader, I began to seek answers to my endless questions.

I researched the early days of the Roman church, later to become that which we now know as the Roman Catholic Church.

I researched the atrocities committed by the RCC.

I have continued to research countless topics of interest, these past 20+ years, one topic usually leading me to the next.

In short, anything that was deemed to be consciousness raising, as well as enlightening, was explored.

A lover of history, I was always interested in the genealogy of my family; so much so that I have spent the last 20+ years dedicated to the pursuit of my ancestry.

In the course of the research, I came to discover that there were a great many native women on both sides of my family.

Suddenly, the terms that I would use ... Mother Earth, Father Sky, Grandfather Sun, Grandmother Moon, Brother Wind and Sister Rain ... made complete sense to me.

I certainly do my best, throughout my day, to assist Mother Earth in the great healing that is needed; anyone can do the same. You begin to heal the planet, first and foremost, by healing yourself.

Growing up in rural Nova Scotia, I was surrounded by trees. I am a lover of birch and pine trees. Living on the west coast of Newfoundland since 1985, I certainly miss the expanse of this wondrous, and life giving, foliage.

The birch is highly adaptive and able to sustain harsh conditions with casual indifference; bright and beautiful, the birch is a pioneer, courageously taking root and starting anew to revive the landscape where no other would before. 297

297

www.whats-your-sign.com/celtic-meaning-birch-tree.html

This can also be seen as a powerful metaphor for our lives in that the birch asks us to philosophically go where no other will go (voluntarily or otherwise) whereby we must take root in new soils and light our lives with the majesty of our very presence, so that others may observe and do likewise. [298]

The spirit of a pine tree is kind and sensitive, soothing to our emotions and always reminding us that we should make decisions from as clear a perspective as possible. [299] The pine tree also reminds us to express our creative energies without feelings of guilt. [300]

I have several resident crows that are forever perched on the tallest tree branches in my backyard; a sight that greets me when I look out the kitchen window. The crow is a spirit animal associated with life mysteries and magic; likewise, if the crow has chosen you as your spirit or totem animal, I have been told that it supports you in developing the power

---

298

www.whats-your-sign.com/celtic-meaning-birch-tree.html
[299] http://spiritlodge.yuku.com/topic/1053/Pine-Tree#.VCCe2_ldVEs
[300] Ibid.

of sight, transformation, and connection with life's magic. [301]

With retirement less than two years away, I am only just beginning to embrace my Mi'kmaq heritage. In keeping, I have also just learned about Chaga Tea, the numerous health benefits of which will simply astound you. [302] [303] [304] [305] [306] [307] [308] [309] [310]

---

[301] www.spiritanimal.info/crow-spirit-animal/

[302] https://chagamountain.com/what-is-chaga/

[303] https://chagamountain.com/chaga-benefits/

[304] https://oriveda.wordpress.com/chaga-the-facts/

[305] https://www.annandachaga.com/

[306] www.fiddleheadheaven.com/chaga-mushrooms.php

[307] https://www.elephantjournal.com/2013/04/chaga-why-this-fungus-is-so-good-for-us-3-delicious-ways-to-reap-its-benefits-catie-joyce/

[308] www.modernroots.org/blog/how-to-make-a-chaga-tincture

[309] www.mindfulyogahealth.com/blog/chaga-superfood-smoothie-recipe

[310] https://chaga101.com/chaga-recipes/

By the time I had entered into my early twenties, I knew that organized religion was no longer for me; instead, I chose to take what resonated with me from a multitude of different approaches.

I had managed to overcome the deep rooted influence of the church to forge my own path in life. As I am continually changing, evolving, BEcoming, so, too, is my paradigm maturing, expanding and unfolding.

As per the prose poem, Desiderata, written by Max Ehrmann in 1927, these are my paraphrased words.

I AM a child of the universe, no less than the trees and the stars, I have a right to be here; and whether or not it is clear to you, no doubt the universe is unfolding, as it should. I AM at peace with God, whatever I conceive him to be. Given my labours and aspirations, in the noisy confusion of life, I AM at peace with my soul. With all its sham, drudgery and broken dreams, this is still a beautiful world. Take the time to strive to be happy.

Throughout this text, I have attempted to resurrect the image of Mary Magdalene, taking the time to show what it is that I believe; namely, that she was an exalted personage.

It is also my belief that the RCC cleverly hid the *real* story of Mary Magdalene; possibly the wife of Yeshua, and the mother to his children, she was seen to be the individual that he trusted above all others.

Is this why a deep disconnect between the true ability of women to be nurturers, healers and mothers, has continued to exist to the present day?

Before the male dominated medical profession took over, women were present at all of the major turning points; namely, birth, sickness and death. In short, women were the healers. As a result, many women were burned at the stake as heretics.

As the Phoenix rises from the ashes, so, too, have I attempted to reclaim my power, rewriting my own story, through copious research and the writing of this book.

It has been a pleasure to but offer you a glimpse into my own spiritual journey, courtesy of comments, thoughts, reflections, understandings and personal meditations.

In Conclusion

While it has been over twenty years since I first embarked on this spiritual journey, in truth, it feels like I have only just begun.

I totally concur with actor Russell Brand when he says that reality is the result of both one's intention and one's attention; we are spiritual beings who have a *daily access to realms of unseen power* as he so intuitively describes. [311]

Consciousness is an ever expanding entity; unfortunately, we allow our consciousness to be prohibited by what we experience within the realm of the five limited senses, the trappings of this material plane.

Whilst housed within these physical bodies, there are other vibrations, frequencies and energies, moving about the universe, to which we do not have access.

---

[311] www.bbncommunity.com/must-watch-russell-brand-destroys-everything-told/

In truth, however, reality is limitless, space is infinite and time is eternal.

We have, within ourselves, an infinite capacity to connect with all things.

We cannot define ourselves in reference to external coordinates; instead, we must learn to define ourselves on an internal level. We are the physical manifestation of a higher frequency, a higher creative force.

When we choose to ignore the spiritual, we create a deficit for ourselves, a deficit for our culture and a deficit for the planet.

We are too quick to identify ourselves as individuals; an idea that is fortified, daily, through the stimulation of prime desires (which further anchor us to the self), and we ignore that fact that we are all connected to each other.

Beneath and beyond our identities as human beings lies the reality of our spirituality; as divine BEings, as a part of the infinite source of creativity, we are connected to all living things.

The definition of God for Russell Brand lies in *recognizing the divine beauty in all of us*. It becomes the focusing on this belief, over our own selfish material needs, then we naturally create a culture more in harmony with selfless connection.

Individualism is a temporary, transient idea.

Individualism is not more important that paganism.

Paganism is the ancestral religion of the whole of humanity; one wherein nature is venerated, everyone is part of Mother Earth, divinity reveals itself in every facet of the world, in every being (man and animal)

Even more important are the things that we all share: love, unity, togetherness.

The current culture narrative suppresses these ideas in favor of negative human traits: greed, selfishness, lust.

This is what keeps us existing in opposition to one another.

This is what keeps corporations exploiting and controlling us.

We are not here to compete with each other.

We are not here to go to war against each other, even though we may be waging an inner war between individualism (ego) and collectivism (oneness).

We are here to remember our divineness, we are here to remember our connectedness and we are here to embrace selfless connection.

Love, compassion, tolerance must become the central tenets of our BEing.

The sooner we acknowledge how common our humanity is, while still appreciating the unity and diversity of the human community, the better off we will be; in truth, we are of the *same* family.

It becomes this very acknowledgement that enables one to feel both humbled and yet very connected.

All truths are easy to understand once they are discovered; the point is to discover them.

Galileo Galilei

Quite simply, we know what we think we know based on what we are (have been) told, courtesy of a myriad of sources; this is why I am always wanting to take a leap of faith, reaching outside the box, outside my comfort zone, to see (feel) what resonates with my own inner truth. This volume has embraced the rediscovery of that truth.

What, then, do you hold as your truth?

Acknowledgments

Close to ten years ago, I had the pleasure of meeting many individuals, courtesy of the Magdalene Line Yahoo Group; namely,

Susan Barefield, an Acadian cousin, who, like myself, is on her own journey of Gnosis, and first alluded me to the possible linkage that may exist between exiled Jews during the time of the Inquisition and French Acadian, French Canadian and Cajun individuals; it seems that DNA testing may be our only answer to this unsolved mystery.

Elsie Nannette Blondet, an inquisitive soul, much like myself, dedicated to finding and sharing the truth; unfortunately, this soul sister transitioned to the other side on January 13, 2010.

Timothy Carmain, for continuing to impart his personal knowledge on questions of both a spiritual and genealogical basis, in the years since our initial meeting; all have been of significant importance to my personal growth.

Madeleine Dubrovsky, whose name is a French derivative of Magdalene; through an ancient form of dance, she, too, is a fellow seeker of the Divine Feminine.

Cris Ann Mulreed, an incredible individual who has meditated with the essential oil of spikenard (courtesy of James Twyman, the Peace Troubador), an oil that has been linked to the Magdalene; as a facilitator of a study group based on the Ask and It Is Given book by Esther and Jerry Hicks, she is very much a believer in the spiritual Law of Attraction.

Suzanne Olsson, author of Jesus in Kashmir: The Lost Tomb; an honor to assist her in the editing of her manuscript, I am ever so thankful for the continued email exchanges, over the years (many in reference to shared genealogy), all of which have led to the most enlightening of conversations that I never expected to have.

Elio Sierra, for continuing to share his extensive knowledge, with remarkable insight, in the years since our initial meeting; in fact, it was back in 2006 that he wrote *as human beings, we cannot force other human beings into doing anything (because of free will), but we have the ability to set an example and to be the light to the world, so to speak, and therefore affect social consciousness.*

This is *exactly* what I have been attempting to do, courtesy of my published works, since 2009.

Gail Heron Sterling, with whom I share a fascination regarding the power, resonance and beauty of contemporary Crystal Skulls; she works with these mediums of the mineral kingdom on an intuitive level, having been introduced to them through Bryan de Flores. Like Cris Ann, she has also meditated with the essential oil of spikenard.

As people come together, one comes to experience the knowledge, and understanding, that it really is an incredibly small world, orchestrated with much synchronicity.

In addition, I wish to impart additional thanks to

Barry Dunford, for permission to reproduce a copy of the wording below the stained glass window as well his photograph of the Kilmore church located in Dervaig on the Scottish western Isle of Mull.

Sabrina Underwood, the Ink Witch, for permission to reproduce a copy of her inspirational Shape of the Elements drawing located in the Personal Meditations section.

John Shuster, for permission to reproduce a copy of his photograph of the stained glass window located in the Kilmore church as located in Dervaig on the Scottish western Isle of Mull.

Book Bibliography

The books that follow herein are those that have served to inspire me on this journey of enlightenment.

Addison, Charles G. (1997) History of the Knights Templar

Ambrose, Kala. (2007) 9 Life Altering Lessons: Secrets of the Mystery Schools Unveiled

Anderson, Sherry and Hopkins, Patricia. (1992) The Feminine Face of God: the Unfolding of the Sacred in Women

Andrews, Richard. (1996) The Tomb of God: The Body of Jesus and The Solution To A 2,000 Year Old Mystery

Arimathea, Joseph of. (1999) The Book of The Holy Grail

Arnold, John. (2001) Inquisition and Power: Catharism and the Confessing Subject in Medieval Languedoc

Ashley-Farrand, Thomas. (2003) Shakti Mantras: Tapping into the Great Goddess Energy Within

Baigent, Michael, Leigh, Richard and Lincoln, Henry. (2004) The Holy Blood and The Holy Grail

Baird, Robert Bruce. (2008) Merovingians: Past and Present Masters

Barber, Malcolm. (2000) The Cathars: Dualist Heretics in Languedoc in the High Middle Ages

Barber, Malcolm. (1993) The Trial of the Templars

Braden, Gregg. (1995) Awakening to Zero Point: The Collective Initiation

Braden, Gregg. (1997) Walking Between the Worlds: The Science of Compassion

Braden, Gregg. (2000) The Isaiah Effect: Decoding the Lost Science of Prayer and Prophecy

Braden, Gregg. (2000) Beyond Zero Point: The Journey to Compassion

Braden, Gregg, (2004) The God Code: The Secret of Our Past, The Promise of Our Future

Braden, Gregg. (2004) <u>The Divine Name: Sounds of the God Code</u> (audio book)

Braden, Gregg. (2005) <u>The Lost Mode of Prayer</u> (audio CD)

Braden, Gregg. (2005) <u>Unleashing The Power of The God Code: The Mystery and Meaning of the Message in Our Cells</u> (audio CD)

Braden, Gregg. (2005) <u>An Ancient Magical Prayer: Insights from the Dead Sea Scrolls</u> (audio book)

Braden, Gregg. (2005) <u>Speaking the Lost Language of God: Awakening the Forgotten Wisdom of Prayer, Prophecy and the Dead Sea Scrolls</u> (audio book)

Braden, Gregg. (2005) <u>Awakening the Power of A Modern God: Unlock the Mystery and Healing of Your Spiritual DNA</u> (audio book)

Braden, Gregg. (2006) <u>Secrets of The Lost Mode of Prayer</u>

Braden, Gregg. (2007) <u>The Divine Matrix: Bridging Time, Space, Miracles and Belief</u>

Bradley, Michael. (1996) <u>Holy Grail Across the Atlantic: The Secret History of Canadian Discovery and Exploration</u>

Bradley, Michael. (1998) <u>Grail Knights of North America: On the Trail of the Grail Legacy in Canada and the United States</u>

Bradley, Michael. (2005) <u>Swords at Sunset: Last Stand of North America's Grail Knights</u>

Bradley, Michael. (2008) <u>The Secrets about the Freemasons</u>

Browne, Sylvia. (2000) <u>God, Creation and Tools for Life</u> (Book 1 of the Journey of the Soul series)

Browne, Sylvia. (2000) <u>Soul's Perfection</u> (Book 2 of the Journey of the Soul series)

Browne, Sylvia. (2001) <u>The Nature of Good and Evil</u> (Book 3 of the Journey of the Soul series)

Browne, Sylvia. (2007) <u>Mother God & Father God</u>

Bunick, Nick. (1998) <u>In God's Truth</u>

Burnham, Sophy. (2002) <u>The Treasure of Montségur: A Novel of the Cathars</u>

Butler, Alan and Dafoe, Stephen. (1999) <u>The Knights Templar Revealed: The Secrets of the Cistercian Legacy</u>

Butler, Alan and Dafoe, Stephen. (2006) <u>The Warriors and the Bankers: A History of the Knights Templar from 1307 to the Present</u>

Cannon, Dolores. (1999) <u>Jesus and the Essenes: Fresh Insight's into Christ's Ministry and the Dead Sea Scrolls</u>

Chopra, Deepak. (1998) <u>The Path to Love: Spiritual Strategies for Healing</u>

Chopra, Deepak. (2005) <u>Peace Is The Way: Bringing War and Violence to An End</u>

Coelho, Paulo. (1998) <u>The Alchemist</u>

Coelho, Paulo. (2003) <u>Warrior Of The Light</u>

Cooper, Adrian P. (2008) <u>Science of Being In Twenty Seven Lessons</u>

Costen, Michael. (1997) <u>The Cathars and The Albigensian Crusade</u>

Cowper, Marcus and Dennis, Peter. (2006) <u>Cathar Castles: Fortresses of the Albigensian Crusade 1209-1300</u>

Craney, Glen. (2008) <u>The Fire and the Light: A Novel of the Cathars and the Lost Teachings of Christ</u>

Crowley, Gary. (2006) <u>From Here to Here: Turning Toward Enlightenment</u>

Dafoe, Stephen. (2007) <u>Nobly Born: An Illustrated History of The Knights Templar</u>

Dafoe, Stephen. (2008) <u>The Compass and the Cross: A History of the Masonic Knights Templar</u>

Das, Lama Surys. (1998) <u>Awakening the Buddha Within</u>

Das, Lama Surys. (2000) <u>Awakening to the Sacred: Creating a Spiritual Life From Scratch</u>

Das, Lama Surys. (2001) <u>Awakening the Buddhist Heart: Integrating Love, Meaning and Connection Into Every Part of Your Life</u>

Das, Lama Surys. (2003) <u>Living Kindness: The Buddha's Ten Guiding Principles for a Blessed Life</u>

Das, Lama Surys. (2003) <u>Letting Go of the Person You Used To Be: Lessons on Change, Loss and Spiritual Transformation</u>

de Vere, Nicholas. (2004) <u>The Dragon Legacy: The Secret History of an Ancient Bloodline</u>

Douzet, André. (2006) <u>The Wandering of the Grail: The Cathars, the Search for the Grail, and the Discovery of Egyptian Relics in the French Pyrenees</u>

Emerys, Chevalier. (2007) <u>Revelation of the Holy Grail</u>

Ford. (2005) <u>Becoming God</u>

Francke, Sylvia. (2007) <u>The Tree of Life and The Holy Grail: Ancient and Modern Spiritual Paths and the Mystery of Rennes-le-Château</u>

Freke, Timothy. (2005) Lucid Living

Freke, Timothy. (2009) How Long Is Now? A Journey to Enlightenment and Beyond

Freke, Timothy, and Gandy, Peter. (2001) The Jesus Mysteries: Was the Original Jesus a Pagan God?

Freke, Timothy, and Gandy, Peter. (2002) Jesus and The Lost Goddess: The Secret Teachings of the Original Christians

Freke, Timothy, and Gandy, Peter. (2006) The Laughing Jesus: Religious Lies and Gnostic Wisdom

Freke, Timothy, and Gandy, Peter. (2007) The Gospel of the Second Coming

Gardiner, Philip and Osborn, Gary. (2006) The Serpent Grail: The Truth Behind the Holy Grail, the Philosopher's Stone and the Elixir of Life

Gardner, Laurence. (2000) Genesis of the Grail Kings: The Explosive Story of Genetic Cloning of and the Ancient Bloodline of Jesus

Gardner, Laurence. (2001) <u>Bloodline of the Holy Grail: The Hidden Lineage of Jesus Revealed</u>

Gardner, Laurence. (2003) <u>Realm of the Ring Lords: The Myth and Magic of the Grail Quest</u>

Gardner, Laurence. (2005) <u>Lost Secrets of the Sacred Ark: Amazing Revelations of the Incredible Power of God</u>

Gardner, Laurence. (2006) <u>The Magdalene Legacy: The Jesus and Mary Bloodline Conspiracy</u>

Gardner, Laurence. (2007) <u>The Shadow of Solomon: The Lost Secret of the Freemasons Revealed</u>

Gardner, Laurence. (2008) <u>The Grail Enigma: The Hidden Heirs of Jesus and Mary Magdalene</u>

Gawain, Shakti. (1993) <u>Living In The Light: A Guide to Personal and Planetary Transformation</u>

Gawain, Shakti. (1999) <u>The Four Levels of Healing</u>

Gawain, Shakti. (2000) <u>The Path of Transformation: How Healing Ourselves Can Change The World</u>

Gawain, Shakti. (2003) <u>Reflections in The Light: Daily Thoughts and Affirmations</u>

Gimbutas, Marija. (1992) <u>The Civilization of the Goddess</u>

Gimbutas, Marija. (2001) <u>The Language of the Goddess</u>

Gimbutas, Marija. (1982) <u>The Goddesses and Gods of Old Europe</u>

Gimbutas, Marija. (2001) <u>The Living Goddesses</u>

Good, Deirdre Joy. (2005) <u>Miriam, the Magdalene and the Mother</u>

Guirdham, Arthur. (2004) <u>The Cathars & Reincarnation</u>

Guirdham, Arthur. (2004) <u>We Are One Another</u>

Guirdham, Arthur. (2004) <u>The Lake and The Castle</u>

Hansard, Christopher. (2003) <u>The Tibetan Art of Positive Thinking</u>

Haskins, Susan. (1994) <u>Mary Magdalene: Myth and Metaphor</u>

Harvey, Andrew and Baring, Anne. (1996) The Divine Feminine

Hassnain, Fida. (2006) The Fifth Gospel: New Evidence from The Tibetan, Sanskrit, Arabic, Persian and Urdu Sources About the Historical Life of Jesus Christ After the Crucifixion

Hicks, Esther and Hicks, Jerry. (2004) Ask and It Is Given: Learning to Manifest Your Desires

Hicks, Esther and Hicks, Jerry. (2005) The Amazing Power of Deliberate Intent: Living the Art of Allowing

Hicks, Esther and Hicks, Jerry. (2006) The Law of Attraction: The Basics of the Teachings of Abraham

Hicks, Esther and Hicks, Jerry. (2008) The Astonishing Power of Emotions: Let Your Feelings Be Your Guide

Hicks, Esther and Hicks, Jerry. (2009) The Vortex: Where The Law of Attraction Assembles all Cooperative Relationships

Hughes, Nita. (2003) <u>Past Recall: When Love and Wisdom Transcend Time</u>

Hughes, Nita. (2006) <u>The Cathar Legacy</u>

Ingram, Julia and Hardin, G.W. (1997) <u>The Messengers: A True Story of Angelic Presence and the Return to the Age of Miracles</u>

Ingram, Julia. (2011) <u>The Lost Sisterhood: The Return of Mary Magdalene, the Mother Mary and Other Holy Women</u>

Jacobovici, Simcha and Pellegrino, Charles. (2008) <u>The Jesus Family Tomb</u>

Jacobovici, Simcha and Wilson, Barrie. (2014) <u>The Lost Gospel: Decoding the Ancient Text that Reveals Jesus' Marriage to Mary the Magdalene</u>

James, John. (2007) <u>The Great Field: Soul At Play In The Conscious Universe</u>

Jansen, Katherine Ludwig. (2001) <u>The Making of the Magdalen: Preaching and Popular Devotion in the Later Middle Ages</u>

Johnson, Bettye. (2005) Secrets of the Magdalene Scrolls: The Forbidden Truth of the Life and Times of Mary Magdalene

Johnson, Bettye. (2007) Mary Magdalene, Her Story

Judd, Isha. (2008) Why Walk When You Can Fly: Soar Beyond Your Fears and Love Yourself and Others Unconditionally

Kenyon, Tom and Sion, Judi. (2006) The Magdalene Manuscript: The Alchemies of Horus and The Sex Magic of Isis

Knight, Christopher and Lomas, Robert. (2001) The Hiram Key: Pharaohs, Freemasonry, and the Discovery of the Secret Scrolls of Jesus

Knight, Christopher and Lomas, Robert. (2001) Second Messiah: Templars, the Turin Shroud and the Great Secret of Freemasonry

King, Karen. (2003) The Gospel of Mary of Magdala: Jesus and the First Woman Apostle

Kinstler, Clysta. (1991) <u>The Moon Under Her Feet</u>

Koven, Jean-Claude. (2004) <u>Going Deeper: How To Make Sense of Your Life When Your Life Makes No Sense</u>

Kribbe, Pamela. (2008) <u>The Jeshua Channelings: Christ Consciousness in a New Era</u>

Laidler, Keith. (1998) <u>The Head of God: The Lost Treasure of The Templars</u>

Laidler, Keith. (2000) <u>The Divine Deception: The Church, The Shroud and The Creation of a Holy Fraud</u>

Lama, Dalai. (2004) <u>The Wisdom of Forgiveness: Intimate Conversations and Journey</u>

Lambert, Malcolm D. (1998) <u>The Cathars</u>

Leloup, Jean-Yves. (2002) <u>The Gospel of Mary Magdalene</u>

Leloup, Jean-Yves. (2006) <u>The Sacred Embrace of Jesus and Mary: The Sexual Mystery at the Heart of the Christian Tradition</u>

Lincoln, Henry. (1997) <u>Key to the Sacred Pattern: The Untold Story of Rennes-le-Château</u>

Lincoln, Henry. (2004) <u>The Holy Place: Sauniere and the Decoding of the Mystery of Rennes-le-Château</u>

Longfellow, Ki. (2007) <u>The Secret Magdalene</u>

Lyons, Lona. (2007) <u>The Magdalene Dispensation</u> (Book 1)

Lyons, Lona. (2008) <u>Daughter of Magdalene</u> (Book 2)

Magdalena, Flo Aeveia. (1992) <u>I Remember Union: The Story of Mary Magdalene</u>

Malachi, Tau. (2006) <u>St. Mary Magdalene: The Gnostic Tradition of the Holy Bible</u>

Malachi, Tau. (2005) <u>Living Gnosis: A Practical Guide to Gnostic Christianity</u>

Manitara, Olivier. (1998) <u>The Essenes: From Jesus to Our Time</u>

Mann, William. (2004) <u>The Knights Templar in the New World: How Henry Sinclair Brought the Grail to Acadia</u>

Mann, William. (2006) <u>The Templar Meridians: The Secret Mapping of the New World</u>

Marjanen, Antti. (1996) <u>The Woman Jesus Loved: Mary Magdalene in the Nag Hammadi Library and Related Documents</u>

Markale, Jean. (2004) <u>The Church of Mary Magdalene: The Sacred Feminine and the Treasure of Rennes-Le-Château</u>

Markale, Jean. (2003) <u>Montségur and The Mystery of the Cathars</u>

Martin, Sean. (2004) <u>The Cathars: The Most Successful Heresy of the Middle Ages</u>

Mattingly, Alan. (2005) <u>Walking in the Cathar Region: Cathar Castles of South West France</u>

Meurois-Givaudan, Anne and Daniel. (1992) <u>The Way of the Essenes</u>

Meyer, Marvin. (2009) <u>The Gospels of Mary: The Secret Tradition of Mary Magdalene, the Companion of Jesus</u>

McTaggart, Lynne. (2003) The Field: The Quest For The Secret Force Of The Universe

McTaggart, Lynne. (2008) The Intention Experiment: Using Your Thoughts to Change Your Life and the World

McTaggart, Lynne. (2011) The Bond: Connecting Through the Space Between Us

Miles, Rosalind. (2002) The Child of the Holy Grail

Millman, Dan. (1990) Way of the Peaceful Warrior

Millman, Dan. (1991) Sacred Journey of the Peaceful Warrior

Millman, Dan. (1992) No Ordinary Moments: A Peaceful Warrior's Guide to Daily Life

Millman, Dan. (1995) The Life You Were Born To Live

Millman, Dan. (1999) Everyday Enlightenment

Moerland, Bram. (2009) The Cathars

Monaghan, Patricia. (1999) The Goddess Companion: Daily Meditations on the Feminine Spirit

Montgomery, Hugh. (2006) The God-Kings of Europe: The Descendants of Jesus Traces Through the Odonic and Davidic Dynasties

Montgomery, Hugh. (2008) The God-Kings of Outremer

Montgomery, Hugh. (2011) The God-Kings of England: The Viking and Norman Dynasties and their Conquest of England (983 - 1066)

Morgan, Marlo. (1994) Mutant Messages Down Under

Morgan, Marlo. (1999) Mutant Messages From Forever: A Novel of Aboriginal Wisdom

Moses, Jeffrey. (2002) Oneness: Great Principles Shared By All Religions

Myss, Caroline. (2001) Sacred Contracts: Awakening Your Divine Potential

Murray, Alexander Callander. (2000) <u>From Roman to Merovingian Gaul: A Reader</u>

Murray, Alexander Callander. (2005) <u>Gregory of Tours: The Merovingians</u>

Nahmad, Claire and Bailey, Margaret. (2006) <u>The Secret Teachings of Mary Magdalene</u>

Nichols, L. Joseph (2000) <u>The Soul As Healer: Lessons in Affirmation, Visualization and Inner Power</u>

Norton, Joan. (2005) <u>The Mary Magdalene Within</u>

Notovitch, Nicolas. (2010) <u>The Unknown Life of Jesus Christ</u>

Oldenbourg, Zoe. (2006) <u>Massacre at Montsegur: A History of the Albigensian Crusade</u>

Olsson, Suzanne. (2005) <u>Jesus in Kashmir, The Lost Tomb</u>

Ortenberg, Veronica. (2006) <u>In Search of The Holy Grail</u>

O'Shea, Stephen (2001) <u>The Perfect Heresy: The Revolutionary Life and Death of the Medieval Cathars</u>

Osman, Ahmed. (2002) <u>Moses and Akhenaten: The Secret History of Egypt at the Time of the Exodus</u>

Osman, Ahmed. (2003) <u>The Hebrew Pharaohs of Egypt: The Secret Lineage of the Patriarch Joseph</u>

Osman, Ahmed. (2004) <u>Jesus in the House of the Pharaohs: The Essene Revelations on the Historical Jesus</u>

Osman, Ahmed. (2005) <u>Christianity: An Ancient Egyptian Religion</u>

Pagels, Elaine. (1989) <u>The Gnostic Gospels</u>

Pagels, Elaine. (1996) <u>The Origin of Satan</u>

Peniel, Jon. (1998) <u>The Lost Teachings of Atlantis: The Children of The Law of One</u>

Peniel, Jon. (1999) <u>The Golden Rule Workbook: A Manual for the New Millennium</u>

Phillips, Graham. (2001) <u>The Marian Conspiracy: The Hidden Truth About the Holy Grail, The Real Father of Christ</u>

Picknett, Lynn and Prince, Clive. (1998) The Templar Revelation: Secret Guardians of the True Identity of Christ

Picknett, Lynn and Prince Clive. (2006) The Sion Revelation: The Truth About the Guardians of Christ's Sacred Bloodline

Picknett, Lynn. (2003) Mary Magdalene: Christianity's Hidden Goddess

Picknett, Lynn and Prince, Clive. (2007) The Turin Shroud: How Da Vinci Fooled History

Pinkham, Mark Amaru. (2004) Guardians of the Holy Grail: The Knights Templar, John the Baptist, and the Water of Life

Radin, Dean I. (2006) Entangled Minds: Extrasensory Experiences in a Quantum Reality

Radin, Dean I. (2009) The Conscious Universe: The Scientific Truth of Psychic Phenomena

Rasha. (1998) The Calling

Rasha. (2006) <u>Oneness</u>

Read, Paul Piers. (1999) <u>The Templars</u>

Redfield, James. (1995) <u>The Celestine Prophecy</u>

Redfield, James. (1997) <u>The Celestine Vision: Living the New Spiritual Awareness</u>

Redfield, James. (1998) <u>The Tenth Insight</u>

Redfield, James. (1999) <u>The Secret of Shambhala</u>

Renard, Gary. (2004) <u>The Disappearance of the Universe</u>

Renard, Gary. (2006) <u>Your Immortal Reality: How To Break the Cycle of Birth and Death</u>

Rennison, Susan Joy. (2008) <u>Tuning the Diamonds: Electromagnetism and Spiritual Evolution</u>

Robinson, John J. (1991) <u>Dungeon, Fire and Sword</u>

Ruiz, Don Miguel. (1997) <u>The Four Agreements: A Practical Guide to Personal Freedom</u>

Ruiz, Don Miguel. (1999) <u>The Mastery of Love: A Practical Guide to The Art of Relationship</u>

Ruiz, Don Miguel. (2000) <u>The Four Agreements Companion Book</u>

Ruiz, Don Miguel. (2004) <u>The Voice of Knowledge: A Practical Guide to Inner Peace</u>

Ruiz, Don Miguel. (2009) <u>Fifth Agreement: A Practical Guide to Self-Mastery</u>

Sams, Jamie. (1994) <u>The 13 Original Clan Mothers</u>

Schaberg, Jane. (2004) <u>The Resurrection of Mary Magdalene: Legends, Apocrypha, and the Christian Testament</u>

Schwartz, Robert. (2009) <u>Your Soul's Plan: Discovering the Real Meaning of the Life You Planned Before You Were Born</u>

Sharma, Robin. (1997) <u>The Monk Who Sold His Ferrari</u>

Sharma, Robin. (2005) <u>Big Ideas to Live Your Best Life: Discover Your Destiny</u>

Shinn, Florence Scovel. (1989) <u>The Wisdom of Florence Scovel Shinn</u>

Shinn, Florence Scovel. (1991) <u>The Game of Life Affirmation and Inspiration Cards: Positive Words For A Positive Life</u>

Shinn, Florence Scovel. (2006) <u>The Game of Life</u> (book and CD)

Simmans, Graham. (2007) <u>Jesus After The Crucifixion: From Jerusalem to Rennes-le-Château</u>

Sjoo, Monica and Mor, Barbara. (1987) <u>The Great Cosmic Mother</u>

Solàrion, Robert. (2005). <u>Apollonius of Tyana and The Shroud of Turin</u>

Sora, Steven. (1999) <u>The Lost Treasure of the Knights Templar: Solving the Oak Island Mystery</u>

Sora, Steven. (2004) Lost Colony of the Templars: Verrazano's Secret Mission to America

Starbird, Margaret. (1998) The Goddess in the Gospels: Reclaiming the Sacred Feminine

Starbird, Margaret. (1993) The Woman with the Alabaster Jar: Mary Magdalene and the Holy Grail

Starbird, Margaret. (2003) Magdalene's Lost Legacy: Symbolic Numbers and the Sacred Union in Christianity

Starbird, Margaret. (2003) The Feminine Face of Christianity

Starbird, Margaret. (2000) The Tarot Trumps and the Holy Grail: Great Secrets of the Middle Ages

Starbird, Margaret. (2005) Mary Magdalene, Bride in Exile

Stone, Merlin. (1978) When God Was a Woman

Stoyanov, Yuri. (2000) The Other God: Dualist Religions from Antiquity to the Cathar Heresy

Strayer, Joseph. (1992) The Albigensian Crusades

Talbot, Michael. (1992) The Holographic Universe

Talbot, Michael. (1993) Mysticism and the New Physics

Tolle, Eckhart. (1999) The Power of Now: A Guide to Spiritual Enlightenment

Tolle, Eckhart. (2001) Practicing the Power of Now: Meditations, Exercises and Core Teachings for Living the Liberated Life

Tolle, Eckhart. (2001) The Realization of Being: A Guide to Experiencing Your True Identity (audio CD)

Tolle, Eckhart. (2003) Stillness Speaks

Tolle, Eckhart. (2003) Entering The Now (audio CD)

Tolle, Eckhart. (2005) A New Earth: Awakening to Your Life's Purpose

Twyman, James. (1998) Emissary of Peace: A Vision of Light

Twyman, James. (2000) The Secret of the Beloved Disciple

Twyman, James. (2000) <u>Portrait of the Master</u>

Twyman, James. (2000) <u>Praying Peace: In Conversation with Gregg Braden and Doreen Virtue</u>

Twyman, James. (2008) <u>The Moses Code: The Most Powerful Manifestation Tool in the History of the World</u>

Twyman, James. (2009) <u>The Kabbalah Code: A True Adventure</u>

Twyman, James. (2009) <u>The Proof: A 40-Day Program for Embodying Oneness</u>

Twyman, Tracy R. (2004) <u>The Merovingian Mythos and the Mystery of Rennes-le-Château</u>

Vasilev, Georgi. (2007) <u>Heresy and the English Reformation: Bogomil-Cathar Influence on Wycliffe, Langland, Tyndale and Milton</u>

Walker III, Ethan. (2003) <u>The Mystic Christ: The Light of Non-Duality and the Path of Love According to the Life and Teachings of Jesus</u>

Walker III, Ethan. (2003) Soft Moon Shining: Poems for the Mother of the Universe

Walker III, Ethan. (2004) Finding God's Love: The Theory and Practice of Love and Devotion As a Spiritual Path

Wallace-Hadrill, J. M. (1982) The Long-Haired Kings and Other Studies in Frankish History

Wallace-Murphy, Tim and Hopkins, Marilyn. (2000) Rosslyn: Guardian of the Secret of the Holy Grail

Wallace-Murphy, Tim; Simmons, Graham and Hopkins, Marilyn. (2000) Rex Deus: The True Mystery of Rennes-le-Château

Wallace-Murphy, Tim and Hopkins, Marilyn. (2007) Templars in America

Wallace-Murphy, Tim. (2008) The Knights of the Holy Grail: The Secret History of the Knights Templar

Walsch, Neale Donald. (1999) Abundance and Right Livelihood: Applications for Living

Walsch, Neale Donald. (2000) <u>Bringers of The Light</u>

Walsch, Neale Donald. (2002) <u>The New Revelations: A Conversation with God</u>

Walters, J. Donald. (2000) <u>Awaken to Superconsciousness: How To Use Meditation for Inner Peace, Intuitive Guidance and Greater Awareness</u>

Walters, J. Donald. (2000) <u>Meditations to Awaken Superconsciousness: Guided Meditations on The Light</u> (audio cassette)

Walters, J. Donald. (2003) <u>Meditation for Starters</u> (book and CD)

Walters, J. Donald. (2003) <u>Metaphysical Meditations</u> (audio CD)

Walters, J. Donald. (2003) <u>Secrets of Bringing Peace On Earth</u>

Weis, Rene. (2002) <u>The Yellow Cross: The Story of the Last Cathar's Rebellion Against the Inquisition, 1290-1329</u>

Weisenthal, Simon. (1998) The Sunflower: On the Possibilities and Limits of Forgiveness

Weiss, Brian. (2001) Messages From The Masters: Tapping into the Power of Love

White, Mary Mageau. Preparing for Ascension e-book (an interactive study course)

White, Mary Mageau. Our Chakra System: A Portal to Interdimensional Consciousness e-book

Wilcock, David. The Shift of the Ages: Convergence Volume One (online book) [312]

Wilcock, David. The Science of Oneness: Convergence Volume Two (online book) [313]

Wilcock, David. The Divine Cosmos: Convergence Volume Three (online book) [314]

---

[312] https://divinecosmos.com/book/18-the-shift-of-the-ages/
[313] https://divinecosmos.com/book/19-the-science-of-oneness/

Wilcock, David. <u>Wanderer Awakening: The Life Story of David Wilcock</u> (online book) [315]

Wilcock, David. <u>The Reincarnation of Edgar Cayce</u> (online book) [316]

Wilcock, David. <u>The End of Our Century</u> (online book edited by David Wilcock) [317]

Wilcock, David. (2011) <u>The Source Field Investigations: The Hidden Science and Lost Civilizations Behind the 2012 Prophecies</u>

Wilcock, David. (2013) <u>The Synchronicity Key: The Hidden Intelligence Guiding the Universe and You</u>

Williamson, Marianne. (1996) <u>A Return To Love</u>

---

[314] https://divinecosmos.com/book/20-the-divine-cosmos/
[315] https://divinecosmos.com/book/25-wander-awakening-the-life-story-of-david-wilcock/
[316] https://divinecosmos.com/book/22-the-reincarnation-of-edgar-cayce-draft-of-pt-1/
[317] https://divinecosmos.com/book/26-the-end-of-our-century/

Williamson, Marianne. (1997) <u>Morning and Evening Meditations and Prayers</u>

Williamson, Marianne. (2002) <u>Everyday Grace: Having Hope, Finding Forgiveness and Making Miracles</u>

Williamson, Marianne. (2003) <u>Being In Light</u> (audio CD set)

Wolf, Fred Alan. (1989). <u>Taking the Quantum Leap: The New Physics for Nonscientists</u>

Wolf, Fred Alan. (2000). <u>Mind Into Matter: A New Alchemy of Science and Spirit</u>

Wolf, Fred Alan. (2002). <u>Matter Into Feeling: A New Alchemy of Science and Spirit</u>

Wolf, Fred Alan. (2004). <u>The Yoga of Time Travel: How the Mind Can Defeat Time</u>

Wolf, Myke. (2010). <u>Create from Being: Guide to Conscious Creation</u>

Wood, David. (1986) <u>Genesis: Book of Revelations</u>

Wood, I. (1995) <u>The Merovingian Kingdoms, 450-751</u>

Wuttunee, Stéphane. <u>Starnations</u>

Wuttunnee, Stéphane. <u>Dreaming the Pyramid</u> e-book

Yogananda, Paramahansa. (1979) <u>Metaphysical Meditations: Universal Prayers, Affirmations and Visualizations</u>

Yogananda, Paramahansa. (2004) <u>The Second Coming of Christ: The Resurrection of the Christ Within You</u>

Young, John K. (2003) <u>Sacred Sites of the Knights Templar: Ancient Astronomers and Freemasons at Stonehenge, Rennes-le-Château and Santiago de Compostela</u>

Zukav, Gary. (1998) <u>The Seat of The Soul</u>

Zukav, Gary. (2001) <u>Thoughts from The Seat of The Soul: Meditations for Souls in Process</u>

Zukav, Gary and Francis, Linda. (2001) <u>The Heart of The Soul: Emotional Awareness</u>

Zukav, Gary and Francis, Linda. (2003) <u>The Mind of The Soul: Responsible Choice</u>

Zukav, Gary and Francis, Linda. (2003) <u>Self-Empowerment Journal: A Companion to The Mind of The Soul: Responsible Choice</u>

Zukav, Gary. (2010) <u>Spiritual Partnership: The Journey to Authentic Power</u>

Website Bibliography

The websites that follow herein are those that have served to guide me in all aspects of my journey of the Sacred Feminine.

ANCIENT CIVILIZATIONS

Ancient Civilizations: Prehistory to Egypt [318]

Before Civilization [319]

Early Human Kinship Was Matrilineal [320]

---

[318]

https://catalogue.pearsoned.co.uk/assets/hip/gb/hip_gb_pear sonhighered/samplechapter/0205161626.pdf

[319]

https://sites.google.com/site/1ancientcivilizationsforkids/anc ient-history-before-civilizations

[320] www.chrisknight.co.uk/wp-content/uploads/2007/09/Early-Human-Kinship-Was-Matrilineal.pdf

APOLLONIUS OF TYANA

Apollonius, Jesus and Paul: Men or Myths? [321]

Apollonius of Tyana [322] [323] [324] [325] [326] [327]

Apollonius of Tyana: A Study of His Life and Times [328]

Apollonius of Tyana's Passage to India [329]

---

[321] www.truthbeknown.com/apollonius.html

[322] www.livius.org/ap-ark/apollonius/apollonius01.html

[323] https://cdn.website-edi-tor.net/e4d6563c50794969b714ab70457d9761/files/uploade d/ApolloniusOfTyana_GRSMead.pdf

[324] www.hermetics.org/pdf/ancient/G.R.S._Mead_-_Apollonius_of_Tyana.pdf

[325] www.chrestos.com/

[326] https://www.alchemylab.com/apollonius.htm

[327] www.wisdomworld.org/setting/apollonius.html

[328] https://ia601200.us.archive.org/16/items/apolloniusoftyan00 cam/apolloniusoftyan00cam.pdf

[329] grbs.library.duke.edu/article/viewFile/1921/3471

Apollonius of Tyana, the Nazarene [330] [331]

Apollonius: The Painful Truth [332]

The Life of Apollonius of Tyana [333] [334] [335]

Turin Shroud: Proof or Doom for Christianity? [336]

BEYOND ME FILMS

As a thinker, creator, innovator, author and teacher, Frank Huguenard has always been intellectually curious; as a result, he had dedicated his life to the understanding and communication of the cross-section of science, religion, spirituality and reality.

---

[330] www.mountainman.com.au/apollonius_the_nazarene_0.htm

[331] members.iimetro.com.au/~hubbca/apollonius.htm

[332] https://hwarmstrong.com/enlyten-apollonius.htm

[333] www.livius.org/ap-ark/apollonius/apollonius_life.html

[334] www.universaltheosophy.com/pdf-library/Life%20of%20Apollonius%20of%20Tyana_FCC.pdf

[335] ryanfb.github.io/loebolus-data/L016N.pdf

[336] https://apolloniustyaneus.blogspot.gr/2013/12/turin-shroud-proof-or-doom-for.html

Huguenard's goal is to make the world better by helping people to nurture their consciousness; he does this by promoting awareness and understanding, distributing enlightenment tools, and encouraging an emphasis on the human soul and consciousness.

Beyond Me [337] provides the missing link between Darwin's Theory of Evolution and the concept of Intelligent Design and offers a simple and practical solution to lifting mankind out of its collective misery.

Beyond Belief [338] takes a look at how certain beliefs about Jesus Christ have been embedded into our collective consciousness and questions their pedigree. All of Modern Christianity hinges on one short document, The Nicene Creed, which is only a few short paragraphs and written some 300 years after the death of Christ. What if they got it wrong?

---

[337] www.beyondmefilm.com/index.php/beyond-me
[338] www.beyondmefilm.com/index.php/beyond-belief

Beyond Reason [339]

The word science comes from the Latin word *scient*, which means "to know" (as in *Omniscient* or "All Knowing"). The spirit of science has always been a quest for the truth: the truth about nature, about the cosmos, about our planet and about ourselves. The Modern Scientific Method, which is a relatively young discipline, has certainly provided mankind with an evolutionary leap in technology and knowhow, but is it the most advanced form of science, in the true essence of the word? Can the Modern Method ever lead us to the *Ultimate Truth*?

BOOKS

The Book of Enoch [340]

The Kabbalah Unveiled [341]

---

[339] www.beyondmefilm.com/index.php/beyond-reason
[340] www.sacred-texts.com/bib/boe/
[341] www.phoenixmasonry.org/kabbalah/index.htm

The Kybalion (The Three Initiates) [342]

The Secret Teachings of All Ages (Manly P. Hall) [343]

CATHARS

Albigensian Crusade [344]

Albigensian Crusade: Online Reference Book for Medieval Studies [345]

Andrew Gough's Arcadia [346]

Brethren Persecuted, Part 1 [347]

----

[342] www.phoenixmasonry.org/kybalion.htm
[343]
www.phoenixmasonry.org/secret_teachings_of_all_ages/table_of_contents.htm
[344] https://en.wikipedia.org/wiki/Albigensian_Crusade
[345] https://www.arlima.net/the-orb/textbooks/crusade/albig.html
[346] www.andrewgough.co.uk/
[347] blog.templarhistory.com/2010/08/brethren-persecuted-part-1/

Brethren Persecuted, Part 2 [348]

Brethren Persecuted, Part 3 [349]

Bogomils and Cathars [350]

Cathar Castles [351]

Cathar Honour [352]

Catharism [353] [354]

Catharism: Should Basic Christianity Be Revived? [355]

---

[348] blog.templarhistory.com/2010/08/brethren-persecuted-part-2/
[349] http://blog.templarhistory.com/2010/08/brethren-persecuted-%E2%80%93-part-3/
[350] https://nullens.org/an-outsiders-view-of-freemasonry/part-a-old-craft/a-6-bogomils-and-cathars/
[351] www.catharcastles.info
[352] www.dhaxem.com/data/handt/Cathar_Honour.pdf
[353] https://en.wikipedia.org/wiki/Catharism
[354] dolphyns.free.fr/English_Version/albigensians.htm
[355] https://hubpages.com/religion-philosophy/Catharism-should-basic-Christianity-be-revived

Catharist Credentes [356]

Cathar Martyrdom: The Cathar View [357]

Cathars [358]

Cathars: A Medieval Tragedy [359]

Cathars and Cathar Beliefs in the Languedoc [360]

Cathars and Reincarnation [361]

Cathar Texts and Rituals [362]

Ceremonies: The Consolamentum [363]

---

[356] https://en.wikipedia.org/wiki/Credentes
[357] www.dhaxem.com/data/handt/Cathar_Martyrdom.pdf
[358] www.mysticmissal.org/cathars.htm
[359] www.computours.net/cathar/
[360] www.cathar.info/
[361] www.innervision.com/mysteries/cathars.html
[362] www.gnosis.org/library/cathtx.htm
[363] www.cathar.info/12011001_consolamentum.htm

Christianity and Its Persecution of the Cathars [364]

Citadels of Vertigo and the Ethics of Desire [365]

City of Béziers Captured By Crusaders [366]

Dhaxem: The Cathar Testament [367]

Gordon Napier History Blog [368]

Kill Them All [369]

Land of the Cathars [370] [371]

---

[364] www.heretication.info/_cathars.html
[365] textualities.net/morelle-smith/citadels-of-vertigo-and-the-ethics-of-desire/
[366] www.burnpit.us/2010/07/city-béziers-captured-crusaders-kill-them-all-god-will-know-his-own
[367] www.dhaxem.com/index.php
[368] gordonnapierhistory.blogspot.com/2010/04/my-first-book-rise-and-fall-of-knights.html
[369] stephenosheaonline.com/kill-them-all/
[370] www.trans4mind.com/counterpoint/index-esoteric/shepherd4.shtml
[371] www.panoccitania.com/cathars.html

Languedoc [372]

Legend of the Cathars [373]

Le Pays Cathare [374]

Manecheism, Catharism and Freemasonry [375]

Massacre at Béziers [376]

Montségur [377 378 379]

Montségur and Carcassonne [380]

---

[372] https://flagspot.net/flags/fr-lr.html
[373] gnosistraditions.faithweb.com/mont.html
[374] https://about-france.com/tourism/cathar-country.htm
[375] www.eleggua.com/Objects/Koulias-Manicheism,_Catharism_and_Freemasonry.html
[376] https://en.wikipedia.org/wiki/Massacre_at_Béziers
[377] www.russianbooks.org/montsegur/montsegur2.htm
[378] www.catharcastles.info/montsegur.php
[379]

www.catharmaiden.com/homepage/pilgrimage/15montsegur.htm
[380]

www.dhaxem.com/data/articles/Montsegur_and_Carcassonne.pdf

Montségur and Its Mysteries [381]

Montségur and The Cathars (Peter Vronsky) [382]

Montségur Photo Tour [383]

Montségur: The Last Bastion of the Cathars [384]

Mysteries of Southern France [385]

Names of Montségur Martyrs [386]

Persecution of the Cathars [387]

Political Background of the Cathar Genocide [388]

---

[381] writingaboutrenneslechateau.blog4ever.com/blog/lire-article-322270-2550617-montsegur_and_its_mysteries.html
[382] www.russianbooks.org/montsegur.htm
[383] https://www.tripsavvy.com/walking-tour-of-montsegur-1517788
[384] http://www.valeriebarrow.com/?p=26
[385] www.innervision.com/mysteries/cathars.html
[386] www.cathar.info/1211b_martyrdom.htm
[387] www.badnewsaboutchristianity.com/gbe_cathars.htm
[388] www.dhaxem.com/data/handt/Catharism_-_Political_Background.pdf

Primary Sources of the Albigensian Crusades [389]

Rebellion and Resistance: The History of Languedoc [390]

Secrets of the Cathars [391] [392]

Siege of Montségur [393]

Simon de Montfort [394]

389

https://artofthetroubadors.wordpress.com/sources/albigensia
n-crusade-primary-sources/
[390] www.creme-de-languedoc.com/Languedoc/history.php
391

https://www.bibliotecapleyades.net/esp_autor_whenry04.ht
m
392

www.hiddenmysteries.org/author/henry/secrets_of_the_cath
ars.pdf
[393] www.russianbooks.org/montsegur/montsegur3.htm
394

https://en.wikipedia.org/wiki/Simon_de_Montfort,_5th_Earl
_of_Leicester

Templars, Cathars and Mary Magdalene, Part 1 [395]

Templars, Cathars and Mary Magdalene, Part 2 [396]

The Albigensian Crusade [397]

The Albigensian Crusade: People, Coinage, Places [398]

The Buzzard: A Short Historical Piece [399]

The Cathar Fortresses [400]

The Cathar Genocide [401]

The Cathar Mantrum [402]

---

[395]

http://gordonnapierhistory.blogspot.com/2010/04/templars-cathars-and-mary-magdalene.html
[396]

http://gordonnapierhistory.blogspot.com/2010/04/templars-cathars-and-mary-magdalene_21.html
[397] www.halexandria.org/dward220.htm
[398] home.eckerd.edu/~oberhot/cathar.htm
[399] www.computours.net/cathar/buzzard.htm
[400] garrenshay.blogspot.com/2011/10/cathar-fortresses.html
[401] www.dhaxem.com/data/handt/Cathar_Genocide.pdf
[402] www.wholisticworldvision.org/inspirations.html

The Cathar Prophecy of 1244 AD [403] [404]

The Cathars [405] [406]

The Cathars, Part 1 [407]

The Cathars, Part 2 [408]

The Cathars and the Albigensian Crusade [409]

The Cathars: Chronology of Events [410]

The Cathars: Les Bons Hommes [411]

---

[403] https://beingatruehuman.wordpress.com/2010/01/15/the-cathar-prophecy-of-1244-ad-the-fountain/
[404] www.oshonews.com/2011/01/the-cathar-prophecy/
[405] ancientquest.com/talks/the-cathars/
[406]

s155239215.onlinehome.us/turkic/50Religion/CatharsEn.htm
[407] www.midihideaways.com/journal/cathars.html
[408] www.midihideaways.com/journal/catharsII.html
[409] https://www.military-history.us/2011/08/the-cathars-and-the-albigensian-crusade/
[410] www.cathar.info/1202b_chronolgy.htm
[411] domainedepalatz.com/en/cathar-country/the-cathars/

The Cathars: The Struggle for, and of, a New Church [412]

The Cathars: Trials and Tribulations in the Languedoc [413]

The Church's War on The Cathars [414] [415]

The Consolamentum [416] [417]

The Crusade Against The Cathars [418]

The Enigma of the Cathars, Part 1 [419]

----

[412]

www.dhaxem.com/data/handt/The_Struggles_for_a_New_Church.pdf
[413] https://www.rosicrucian.org/podcast/the-cathars-trials-and-tribulations-in-the-languedoc-bill-anderson/
[414]

www.dhaxem.com/data/handt/The_Church_War_on_the_Cathars.pdf
[415] https://www.bibliotecapleyades.net/esp_cataros_07.htm
[416] gnosis.org/library/Consolamentum.html
[417] https://templarpriests.weebly.com/consolamentum.html
[418] mescladis.free.fr/ANGLAIS/pages%20html/crusade.htm
[419] templeofpegasus.blogspot.com/2008/08/enigma-of-cathars-part-one.html

The Enigma of the Cathars, Part 2 [420]

The Enigma of the Cathars, Part 3 [421]

The Enigma of the Cathars, Part 4 [422]

The Enigma of the Cathars, Part 5 [423]

The Enigma of the Cathars, Epilogue [424]

The Forgotten Kingdom: The Tragedy of the Cathars [425]

The Great Mysteries of the Languedoc [426]

---

[420] templeofpegasus.blogspot.com/2008/08/enigma-of-cathars-part-two.html
[421] templeofpegasus.blogspot.com/2008/08/enigma-of-cathars-part-three.html
[422] templeofpegasus.blogspot.com/2008/09/enigma-of-cathars-part-four.html
[423] templeofpegasus.blogspot.com/2008/09/enigma-of-cathars-part-five.html
[424] templeofpegasus.blogspot.com/2008/09/enigma-of-cathars-epilogue.html
[425] https://music.douban.com/review/2860158/
[426] www.languedocmysteries.info

The Hidden History of The Secret Church [427]

The Knights Templar: The Cathar Connection [428]

The Legend of the Cathars [429]

The Lessons of the Albigensian Crusades [430]

The Magdalene of the Heretics, Part 1 [431]

The Magdalene of the Heretics, Part 2 [432]

The Martyrdom of the Cathars [433]

---

[427] https://www.gnostic.info/2018/03/31/hidden-history-of-the-secret-church/
[428] www.dhaxem.com/data/handt/Knights_Templar.pdf
[429] https://www.bibliotecapleyades.net/esp_cataros_03.htm
[430] webzine.thesocialedge.com/columns/the-lessons-of-the-albigensian-crusade/
[431] www.templeofmysteries.com/mary-magdalene/the-magdalene-of-the-heretics-part-i.php
[432] www.templeofmysteries.com/mary-magdalene/the-magdalene-of-the-heretics-part-ii.php
[433] https://www.trekearth.com/gallery/Europe/France/South/Midi-Pyrenees/Montsegur/photo286675.htm

The Medieval Inquisition in the Languedoc [434]

The Medieval Roman Inquisition [435]

The Perfect Heresy [436]

The Perfect Heretics [437]

The Pure Ones [438]

The Rise of Heresies and Catholic Responses [439]

The Voice of the Cathars, Part 1 (by Louis Khourey) [440]

The Voice of the Cathars, Part 2 (by Louis Khourey) [441]

---

[434] www.cathar.info/1209_inquisition.htm

[435] www.dhaxem.com/data/handt/Medieval_Roman_Inquisition.pdf

[436] www.briancreese.co.uk/cathars.htm

[437] www.playbackarts.co.uk/meryfela/perfect.htm

[438] https://www.bibliotecapleyades.net/esp_cataros_06.htm

[439] www.gutenberg-e.org/maclehose/appendix2.html

[440] tatfoundation.org/forum2001-06.htm#5

[441] tatfoundation.org/forum2001-07.htm#5

The Voice of the Cathars, Part 3 (by Louis Khourey) [442]

The Walls of Carcassonne [443]

The Wooden Book of Montségur [444]

Wars against the Cathars of the Languedoc (by Voltaire) [445]

What Makes a Cathar? [446]

Who Are The Cathars? [447]

Who Went On The Albigensian Crusades? [448]

Zarathushtra, Mani, and the Cathars [449]

---

[442] tatfoundation.org/forum2001-08.htm#3

[443] www.kellscraft.com/Navarre/OldNavarreCh09.html

[444] https://www.eyeofthepsychic.com/woodenbook/

[445] www.languedoc-france.info/articles/t_voltairecathars.htm

[446] www.dhaxem.com/data/handt/What_makes_a_Cathar.pdf

[447] www.sullivan-county.com/id2/gnostic_files/cather.htm

[448]

https://academic.oup.com/ehr/article/128/534/1047/436468

[449] san.beck.org/GPJ8-ManiandCathars.html

CHRISTIANITY

Arianism versus Catholicism: The Struggle for Power [450]

Christianity and the Roman Empire [451]

Conflict, Consensus, and the Cross: Christianity and its Role in State Politics [452]

Constantine Converts to Christianity [453]

Constantine's Vision [454]

---

[450] www.jesusneverexisted.com/arianism.html

[451] www.bbc.co.uk/history/ancient/romans/christianityromanempire_article_01.shtml

[452] ssp.ucr.edu/files/GregoryGoalwin.pdf

[453] www.thenagain.info/webchron/easteurope/ConstantineConverts.html

[454] https://www.christianhistoryinstitute.org/study/module/constantine/

How Christianity Was Invented [455]

Legitimization Under Constantine [456]

Questions about the Church and History [457]

The DaVinci Code Fraud [458]

The Real History of Christianity [459]

DIVINE FEMININE / SOPHIA

Ecclesia Pistis Sophia (an online community of Sophian Gnostic Fellowship) [460]

---

[455] https://beyondallreligion.net/2012/01/21/how-christianity-was-invented/
[456]

https://www.pbs.org/wgbh/pages/frontline/shows/religion/why/legitimization.html
[457] www.denverchristadelphians.org/davinci/History.htm
[458] www.philvaz.com/apologetics/DaVinciCode.htm
[459]

https://www.bibliotecapleyades.net/esp_biblianazar.htm#inicio
[460] www.sophian.org/

Iona: Sacred Isle of the West (Barry Dunford) [461]

Khokhmah and Sophia [462]

Retrieving the Myth of Jesus and Sophia, Part I [463]

Retrieving the Myth of Jesus and Sophia, Part II [464]

Searching for the Divine Feminine: Looking for Aspects of Her Between the Lines [465]

Sophia [466]

Sophia Foundation of North America [467]

Sophia, Goddess of Wisdom [468]

---

[461] sacredconnections.co.uk/index.php/iona-sacred-isle/
[462] www.suppressedhistories.net/articles/sophia.html
[463] www.patheos.com/blogs/aidankelly/2013/11/retrieving-the-myth-of-jesus-and-sophia-part-i/
[464] www.patheos.com/blogs/aidankelly/2013/11/retrieving-the-myth-of-jesus-and-sophia-part-ii/
[465] www.soulfulliving.com/divinefeminine.htm
[466] www.thaliatook.com/AMGG/sophia.php
[467] sophiafoundation.org
[468] www.crystalinks.com/sophia.html

Sophia: Goddess of Wisdom and God's Wife [469]

Sophia's Children: Beautiful Madonna and Mary Magdalene [470]

Speaking of Sophia and the Magdalene: Interview with Tau Malachi [471]

The Bridal Chamber [472]

The Centrality of the Divine Feminine in Sufism [473]

The Divine Feminine [474]

The Divine Feminine (Anne Baring) [475]

---

[469] northernway.org/sophia.html
[470] femininemojo.typepad.com/ssww/2012/05/beautiful-madonna-mary-magdalene.html
[471] https://www.theosophical.org/publications/1529
[472] www.angelfire.com/dc/universalism/bridalchamber.html
[473] www.seekeraftertruth.com/abdullah-muzaffer-laurence-galian-the-centrality-of-the-divine-feminine-in-sufism/
[474] www.theharmonyproject.org/feminine.html
[475] www.annebaring.com/anbar06_div-fem.htm

The Gnostic Goddess, Female Power and the Fallen Sophia
[476]

The Goddess Art of Jonathon Earl Bowser [477]

The Heart of Love [478]

The Pagan Origins of the Gnostic Sophia [479]

The Pistis Sophia: An Introduction [480]

The Spiritual Meaning Behind the Story of Sophia [481]

The Triple Goddess: The Original Holy Trinity [482]

---

[476]
https://www.suppressedhistories.net/articles/GnosticGoddessFallenSophia.pdf
[477] www.jonathonart.com/intro.html
[478] www.theheartoflove.com/
[479] https://thegodabovegod.com/pagan-origins-gnostic-sophia/
[480] https://www.theosophical.org/publications/quest-magazine/2395
[481] https://thegodabovegod.com/spiritual-meaning-behind-story-sophia/
[482] www.mother-god.com/triple-goddess.html

ESSENES

Ancient Essenes [483]

Essene Church of Christ [484]

Essene Gospels of Peace [485] [486]

Nazirene Home Page [487]

The Nazarene Way [488]

The Nazorean Essenes of Mount Carmel [489]

---

[483] www.sevenfoldpeace.com/essenes.html

[484] www.essene.org

[485]

www.thenazareneway.com/index_essene_gospels_of_peace.htm

[486] www.essene.com/GospelOfPeace/

[487] nazirene.org/main.htm

[488]

www.thenazareneway.com/index.htm#The_Descendants_and_Bloodline_of_Christ

[489] www.essene.com

The Real Jesus and the Other Story [490]

GNOSTICISM

Gnosticism, Christianity and Sophia [491]

Gnostic Scriptures and the Gnostic Church [492]

Introduction to Sophian Gnosticism Study Guide [493]

The Gnostic Goddess, Female Power and the Fallen Sophia [494]

The Gnostic Jesus [495]

_____

[490]

mastermason.com/hiramdiscovered/jesusdiscovered1.html
[491]

https://www2.kenyon.edu/Depts/Religion/Projects/Reln91/Gender/Gnosticism.htm
[492] gnosis.org/gnscript.html
[493] http://www.magdalene-circle.org/Sophian_Gnostic_Tradition_Study_Guide.pdf
[494]

https://www.suppressedhistories.net/articles/GnosticGoddessFallenSophia.pdf
[495] www.gnostic-jesus.com

Mary Magdalene: A Personal Connection

The Gnostic Order of Christ [496]

The Lost Gospel of Judas [497]

GODDESS WORSHIP

Anatomy of a Backlash: Concerning the Work of Marija Gimbutas [498]

Ancient Mother Goddesses and Fertility Cults [499]

Ancient Wisdom: Earth – Mother – Earth [500]

History versus the DaVinci Code [501]

---

[496] www.gnosticorderofchrist.org
[497] www.nytimes.com/packages/pdf/national/judastxt.pdf
[498]

www.charlenespretnak.com/files/JoA_article_by_CS_on_M G.pdf
[499]

https://jarm.journals.yorku.ca/index.php/jarm/article/view/4 952
[500] www.ancient-wisdom.co.uk/earthmother.htm
[501]

www.historyversusthedavincicode.com/chaptertwentyeight. htm

267

Justice and the Face of the Great Mother [502]

Knocking Down Straw Dolls (A Critique of Cynthia Eller's The Myth of Matriarchal Prehistory) [503]

Marija Gimbutas: Archaeologist of the Goddess [504]

Meanings of Matriarchy [505]

Mother Cultures and Patriarchal Indo-Europeans [506]

Prehistoric Goddess-Based Cultures [507]

Signs Out Of Times: The Story of Archaeologist Marija Gimbutas [508] [509]

----

[502] https://www.bu.edu/wcp/Papers/Comp/CompGian.htm
[503]

https://www.suppressedhistories.net/articles/strawdolls.html
[504] marijagimbutas.com/
[505] eve.enviroweb.org/perspectives/issues/matriarc.html
[506]

www.lebtahor.com/HB/baggage/mother%20cultures%20and%20pie.htm
[507]

www.opuslibros.org/Index_libros/Recensiones_1/eisler.htm
[508] www.belili.org/marija/aboutSIGNS.html

Story Is Only Part of History: Re-evaluating the Work of Marija Gimbutas [510]

The Beginnings of Patriarchy in Europe: Reflections on the Kurgan Theory of Marija Gimbutas [511]

The Cult of the Mother Goddess [512]

The Great Goddess and Her Influence on Herstorically and in the Present [513]

The Life and Work of Archaeologist Marija Gimbutas [514]

The Myth of Matriarchal Prehistory (Cynthia Eller) [515]

---

[509] https://www.youtube.com/watch?v=BjE2-H1R9Zs

[510] https://www.academia.edu/1117577/Story_Is_Only_Part_of_History_Re-evaluating_the_Work_of_Marija_Gimbutas

[511] www.belili.org/marija/marler_article_02.pdf

[512] https://ericwedwards.wordpress.com/2013/07/17/the-cult-of-the-mother-goddess/

[513] https://www.goddess-pages.co.uk/blog/2006/10/31/the-great-goddess-and-her-influence-herstorically-and-in-the-present-2/

[514] www.midwifingdeath.com/Gimbutas.pdf

[515] https://www.nytimes.com/books/first/e/eller-myth.html

The Myth of Universal Patriarchy (A Critical Response to Cynthia Eller's The Myth of Matriarchal Prehistory) [516]

The World of the Goddess - Marija Gimbutas [517]

Understanding Marija Gimbutas [518]

HOLY GRAIL

Alchemy, Exploring the Spiritual Foundation of Harry Potter [519]

Alchemy Lab [520]

A Seeker's Thoughts on The Holy Grail [521]

CIRCES International [522]

---

[516] www.belili.org/marija/eller_response.html

[517] https://www.youtube.com/watch?v=yU1bEmq_pf0

[518] w.originsnet.org/kbjh.pdf

[519] harrypotterforseekers.com/alchemy/alchemy.php

[520] https://www.alchemylab.com

[521] www.aseekersthoughts.com/2009/01/holy-grail.html

[522] circesinternational.org

From Ritual to Romance [523]

<u>Holy Blood, Holy Grail</u> [524]

Lecture 8: An Alchemical Quest (Anne Baring) [525]

Philosopher's Stone [526]

Royal Marriage: The Marriage of Inner and Outer Worlds [527]

Science of Wholeness is Your Highest Fulfillment [528]

Spiritual Alchemy [529]

The Alchemy Key [530]

---

[523] www.sacred-texts.com/neu/frr/

[524] https://archive.org/details/HolyBloodholyGrail

[525] www.annebaring.com/anbar12_lect08_alchemical.htm

[526] www.occultopedia.com/p/philosophers_stone.htm

[527] https://jungiangenealogy.weebly.com/royal-marriage.html

[528] scienceofwholeness.com/end-suffering/

[529] spiritualalchemy.iwarp.com

[530] www.hermetics.org/pdf/alchemy/Alchemy_Key.pdf

The CASTLE Principles [531]

The Grail Quest [532]

The Grail Quest and The Destiny of Man (of which there are 16 parts) [533]

The High History of the Holy Grail [534] [535]

The International Order of Gnostic Templars [536]

The Movie *The Da Vinci Code*: A Qabalistic Rosicrucian Perspective [537]

The Quest for the Holy Grail [538] [539]

---

[531] https://www.slideshare.net/secretan/castle-principles
[532] www.angelfire.com/in4/alchemy2084/grail.html
[533] https://cassiopaea.org/category/volumes/the-grail-quest-and-the-destiny-of-man/
[534] www.lundyisleofavalon.co.uk/texts/hhothg/index.htm
[535] www.sangraal.com/histgrail.htm
[536] www.gnostictemplars.org/iogtinfo.html
[537] www.lightparty.com/Spirituality/DaVinciCode.html
[538] https://livingnow.com.au/articles/living-and-learning/the-quest-for-the-holy-grail
[539] www.returnofthechrist.org.uk/holy-grail.html

The Ninth Century and The Holy Grail [540]

Trusting Ourselves: Letting Go Of Authority [541]

What is the Holy Grail, really? [542]

JAINISM

An Indian religion (traditionally known as Jaina dharma) that prescribes a path of non-violence towards all living beings and emphasizes spiritual independence and equality between all forms of life; practitioners believe that non-violence and self-control are the means by which they can obtain liberation.

One of the most important and fundamental doctrines of Jainism is anēkāntavāda, a doctrine that refers to [1] the principles of pluralism [543] [544] and multiplicity of viewpoints,

---

540

www.skylarkbooks.co.uk/Shop/media/The_Ninth_Century_ and_the_Holy_Grail_Stein.htm

[541] nolabelsnolies.com/tag/what-is-truth/

[542] www.ariadnegreen.com/holygrail.html

[543] https://en.wikipedia.org/wiki/Pluralism_(philosophy)

[544] https://www.youtube.com/user/PluralismProject

[2] the notion that truth and reality are perceived differently from diverse points of view, and [3] that no single point of view is the complete truth.

Mahatma Gandhi was deeply influenced by Jainism; he proclaimed that the duty of every individual was to determine what is personally true and act on that relative perception of truth.

He also stated that one is duty bound to act according to his relative truth, but at the same time, he is also equally bound to learn from truth as held by his opponent.

Jainism [545] [546] [547] [548] [549] [550] [551]

---

[545] www.jainism.org

[546] www.sacred-texts.com/jai/

[547] www.patheos.com/library/jainism.html

[548] www.bbc.co.uk/religion/religions/jainism/

[549] www.cs.colostate.edu/~malaiya/jainhlinks.html

[550] www.religionfacts.com/jainism

[551]

www.umich.edu/~umjains/jainismsimplified/jainsimp.html

Jain Philosophy [552]

JESUS

A question that has plagued biblical scholars and historians for centuries is why Lucius Mestrius Plutarchus, aka Plutarch the Greek historian, wrote nothing about Jesus or Christianity. [553]

Born about 45 AD, he lived in the midst of the most successful groups and churches determined to bring the new religion to the Greco-Roman world. [554]

His Pythagorean philosophy mirrored the lifestyle and doctrine of Jesus and his closest disciples; in keeping, he would have been profoundly interested in the acts and movements of someone who was teaching Pythagorean philosophy to Jewish communities. [555]

---

[552] https://www.iep.utm.edu/jain/
[553]

www.thenazareneway.com/Plutarch%20and%20Luke.htm
[554] Ibid.
[555] Ibid.

He was famous during his own lifetime for writing biographies and histories of people whose lives impacted the Roman Empire and the Mediterranean world. [556]

Did Jesus Visit Scotland? (Barry Dunford) [557]

Forgery in Christianity [558]

Jesus, A Humble Prophet of God [559]

Jesus and the Christos: A Gnostic Perspective [560]

Jesus in India? The Myth of the Lost Years [561]

---

[556]

www.thenazareneway.com/Plutarch%20and%20Luke.htm
[557] sacredconnections.co.uk/index.php/did-jesus-visit-scotland/
[558]

https://infidels.org/library/historical/joseph_wheless/forgery_in_christianity/
[559] https://www.alislam.org/topics/jesus/
[560] www.llewellyn.com/journal/article/502
[561] www.truthbeknown.com/jesus_in_india.htm

Jesus' Marriage to Mary Magdalene is Fact, Not Fiction [562]

Legends of Jesus [563]

More Dramatic Proof that Jesus and Mary Magdalene Were Married [564]

O Father-Mother Birther of the Cosmos [565]

Revealing the Pesher of Christ: The Relations of Jesus [566]

The Aramaic New Testament [567]

The Gnostic Jesus [568]

---

[562] https://www.huffingtonpost.com/simcha-jacobovici/jesus-marriage-to-mary-th_b_6225826.html
[563] www.tjresearch.info/legends.htm
[564] blogs.timesofisrael.com/more-dramatic-proof-that-jesus-and-mary-magdalene-were-married/
[565] aramaicnt.org/2007/06/09/o-father-mother-birther-of-the-cosmos/
[566] www.pesherofchrist.com/JesusRelations.html
[567] aramaicnt.org/2010/03/07/victor-alexanders-aramaic-bible-translation-or-how-to-tell-apart-syriac-from-galilean-aramaic/
[568] www.gnostic-jesus.com/index.html

The Life and Philosophy of Pythagoras [569]

The Lord's Prayer in Galilean Aramaic [570]

The Lost Years of Jesus: The Life of Saint Issa [571]

The Missing Years of Jesus Documentary [572]

The Original Aramaic Lord's Prayer is None of the Above [573]

The True Jesus and Mary Magdalene [574]

---

[569] www.phoenixmasonry.org/secret_teachings_of_all_ages/the_life_and_philosophy_of_pythagoras.htm

[570] aramaicnt.org/articles/the-lords-prayer-in-galilean-aramaic/

[571] https://reluctant-messenger.com/issa.htm

[572] https://topdocumentaryfilms.com/missing-years-jesus/

[573] www.patheos.com/blogs/exploringourmatrix/2012/02/the-original-aramaic-lords-prayer-is-none-of-the-above.html

[574] www.thetruejesus.org/index.html

The True Story of the Real Jesus [575]

Was Jesus Christ married? [576]

Were Jesus and Mary Magdalene on the Holy Isle of Iona? (Barry Dunford) [577]

MALE AND FEMALE

Male and Female Energies [578]

Masculine and Feminine Energies [579]

Re-Balancing the Masculine and the Feminine (Anne Baring) [580]

Two Energies, One Body [581]

---

[575] http://www.nazoreans.com/index.html
[576] www.benhammott.com/was_jesus_married_news.html
[577] sacredconnections.co.uk/index.php/jesus-and-mary-magdalene-on-iona/
[578] www.jeshua.net/healing/healing5.htm
[579] www.fromthestars.com/page128.html
[580] www.annebaring.com/anbar12_lect05_mascfemine.htm
[581] ezinearticles.com/?Two-Energies,-One-Body---Balance-Your-Male---Female-Sides&id=1134753

MARY MAGDALENE

A Crack in the DaVinci Code [582]

Da Vinci's Code [583]

Jesus and Mary Magdalene: The Sacred Marriage in Gnosticism [584]

Magdalineage [585]

Mary Magdalene [586]

Mary Magdalene and the Voice of Silence [587]

Mary Magdalene: Goddess in the Gospels [588]

---

[582] www.mythomorph.com/wp/a-crack-in-the-da-vinci-code/
[583] witcombe.sbc.edu/davincicode/contents-schedule.html
[584] www.llewellyn.com/journal/article/659
[585] magdalineage.com/
[586] shekinah.elysiumgates.com/magdalene.html
[587] https://www.theosophical.org/publications/1531
[588] northernway.org/mmag.html

Mary Magdalene, the Gospels and the Church [589]

Order of Mary Magdala [590]

Putting the Goddess, the Sacred Feminine, back into Judeo-Christianity [591]

Sacred Union in Christianity (Margaret Starbird) [592]

Secrets of the Magdalene Scroll (Bettye Johnson) [593]

The Gnostic Church of Mary Magdalene [594]

The Gospel of Mary Magdalene and Her Near-Death Experience [595]

---

[589] witcombe.sbc.edu/davincicode/gregory-homily33.html
[590] northernway.org/school/omm.shtml
[591] northernway.org/restore.html
[592] www.margaretstarbird.net/
[593] secretsofthemagdalenescrolls.blogspot.com
[594] noreah.typepad.com/gnostic/
[595] https://www.near-death.com/reincarnation/history/gospel-of-mary.html

The Maeve Chronicles (Elizabeth Cunningham) [596]

The Magdalene Connection [597]

The Magdalene Line (Kathleen McGowan) [598]

The Murder of Mary Magdalene and the Hidden Encryption in Art [599]

The Renaissance of Mary Magdalene [600]

The Secret Magdalene (Ki Longfellow) [601]

Why She Matters So [602]

---

[596] elizabethcunninghamwrites.com/books1

[597] http://www.metahistory.org/MM/MMConnectionOne.php

[598] www.kathleenmcgowan.com

[599] blog.world-mysteries.com/strange-artifacts/the-murder-of-mary-magdalene-and-the-hidden-encryption-in-art/

[600] www.mmagdalene.org

[601] thesecretmagdalene.com

[602] www.metahistory.org/MM/WhySheMatters.php

MĀTĀ AMRITĀNANDAMAYĪ DEVĪ

The Indian saint known as Ammachi, Amma, Mother of Immortal Bliss, and The Hugging Saint; she is a remarkable contemporary woman.

In October of 2002, Ammachi was awarded the prestigious international Ghandi-King Award (named after Mahatma Ghandi and Martin Luther King); an award that is given each year to the person who has contributed the most to non-violence.

Amma (Ashram Headquarters) [603]

Amma (Europe site) [604]

Amma (US site) [605]

Amrita University [606]

---

[603] https://www.amritapuri.org
[604] https://www.amma-europe.org
[605] https://amma.org
[606] https://www.amrita.edu

IAM Technique: Integrated Amrita Meditation Technique [607]

METAPHYSICS

Spirit Science [608]

Spirit Science series (complete episodes) [609]

Spirit, Science and Metaphysics [610]

MINDFULNESS

9 Ways To Deepen Your Mindfulness [611]

10 Easy Ways You Can Practice Mindfulness Every Day [612]

---

[607] https://www.iam-meditation.org
[608] thespiritscience.net
[609] https://www.youtube.com/watch?v=IaDOkMEK4uk
[610]

https://www.facebook.com/SpiritualScienceAndMetaphysics/
[611] https://upliftconnect.com/nine-ways-deepen-mindfulness/
[612] themindunleashed.com/2015/11/10-easy-ways-you-can-practice-mindfulness-every-day.html

Greater Good Science Centre [613]

Harvard University: Mindfulness Meditation [614]

How Mindfulness Empowers Us [615]

How to Develop a Daily Mindfulness Practice (Gelong Thubten) [616]

How To Practice Mindful Self-Compassion [617]

Mindfulness [618]

Mindfulness Everyday [619]

---

[613]
https://greatergood.berkeley.edu/topic/mindfulness/definitio
n
[614] https://news.harvard.edu/gazette/tag/mindfulness-
meditation/
[615] https://upliftconnect.com/mindfulness-empowers-us/
[616] https://www.youtube.com/watch?v=PYD-Gx_9K_M
[617] https://lonerwolf.com/mindful-self-compassion/
[618]
www.vipassana.com/meditation/mindfulness_in_plain_engli
sh_15.php
[619] www.mindfulnesseveryday.org

Mindfulness Exercises [620]

Mindfulness: Finding Peace in a Frantic World [621]

Mindfulness Meditation Benefits: 20 Reasons Why It's Good For Your Mental And Physical Health [622]

Mindfulness Research [623]

Mindfulness Without Borders [624]

Minding Your Own Business [625]

Mindful Schools [626]

The Mindfulness Bell [627]

---

[620] youth.anxietybc.com/mindfulness-exercises

[621] franticworld.com

[622] https://www.huffingtonpost.ca/entry/mindfulness-meditation-benefits-health_n_3016045

[623] https://www.huffingtonpost.com/news/gps-mindfulness-research/

[624] https://mindfulnesswithoutborders.org/

[625] https://www.youtube.com/watch?v=VfzBGoGuYeI

[626] https://www.mindfulschools.org

[627] https://www.mindfulnessbell.org

The Mindfulness Institute [628]

NOVUS SPIRITUS

God the Female [629]

God the Male [630]

PIERRE TEILHARD DE CHARDIN

American Teilhard Association (ATA) [631]

Association des Amis de Pierre Teilhard de Chardin [632]

Cosmogenesis and Consciousness [633]

Religion, Science and Mysticism in Pierre Teilhard de Chardin [634]

---

[628] www.mindfulnessinstitute.ca
[629] www.novus.org/home/godfemale.cfm
[630] www.novus.org/home/godmale.cfm
[631] www.teilharddechardin.org
[632] https://www.teilhard.fr
[633] https://www.huffingtonpost.com/dave-pruett/cosmogenesis-and-consciou_b_4084855.html
[634] www.earthlight.org/essay39_king.html

Teilhard for Beginners [635]

The British Teilhard Association [636]

The Future of Man by Pierre Teilhard de Chardin [637]

The Teilhard de Chardin Project [638]

SANGRÉAL

Recovering the Cosmic Science of Antiquity, Part 1 [639]

Recovering the Cosmic Science of Antiquity, Part 2 [640]

Recovering the Cosmic Science of Antiquity, Part 3 [641]

---

[635] www.teilhardforbeginners.com
[636] https://www.teilhard.org.uk
[637] https://archive.org/details/TheFutureOfMan
[638] www.teilhardproject.com
[639] sacredgeometryinternational.com/sangreal-the-holy-grail-recovering-the-cosmic-science-of-antiquity-part-one
[640] sacredgeometryinternational.com/sangreal-the-holy-grail-recovering-the-cosmic-science-of-antiquity-part-two
[641] sacredgeometryinternational.com/sangreal-the-holy-grail-recovering-the-lost-science-of-antiquity-part-3

Recovering the Cosmic Science of Antiquity, Part 4 [642]

Recovering the Cosmic Science of Antiquity, Part 5 [643]

Sacred Geometry International (SGI) Blog [644]

TEMPLAR KNIGHTS

A History and Mythos of the Knights Templar [645]

Early Christian Mysteries Lecture Series (Andrew Linnell) [646]

Chinon Parchment [647] [648]

---

[642] sacredgeometryinternational.com/sangreal-the-holy-grail-recovering-the-cosmic-science-of-antiquity-part-4
[643] sacredgeometryinternational.com/sangreal-the-holy-grail-recovering-the-lost-science-of-antiquity-part-5
[644] sacredgeometryinternational.com/category/sgi-blog-news
[645] blog.templarhistory.com/category/history/
[646] thechristianmysteries.com/wp-content/uploads/2014/07/Lecture-6-Early-Christian-Mysteries.pdf
[647] www.inrebus.com/chinon.php
[648] https://en.wikipedia.org/wiki/Chinon_Parchment

Forget The DaVinci Code: This is the Real Mystery of the Knights Templar [649]

Friday the 13th and the Knights Templar [650]

Gordon Napier History Blog [651]

Knights Templar [652] [653] [654]

Knights Templar History [655]

New Order of the Knights Templar and the Daughters of Tsion [656]

---

[649] https://templars.wordpress.com/2014/07/29/forget-the-da-vinci-code-this-is-the-real-mystery-of-the-knights-templar/
[650] michaelspradlin.com/blog/2013/09/friday-the-13th-and-the-knights-templar/
[651] gordonnapierhistory.blogspot.com/2010/04/my-first-book-rise-and-fall-of-knights.html
[652] www.lordsandladies.org/knights-templar.htm
[653] www.medieval-life-and-times.info/crusades/knights-templar.htm
[654] www.halexandria.org/dward219.htm
[655] grigorfedan.com/main/Knights_Templar_History
[656] northernway.org/school/templars.html

Processus contra Templarios (Proceedings against the Templars) [657] [658]

Templar Knight 1 [659]

Templar Knight 2 [660]

Templars: The Rise, Fall and Survival of the Knights Templar [661]

The Ancient Symbol of the Knights Templar's Red Cross [662]

---

[657] https://www.youtube.com/playlist?list=PLKtdhxC-9ySJZ-4lBdn10afebtbtq8U37

[658] knightstemplarvault.com/processus-contra-templarios/

[659] www.metatronminutes.net/BBS_Radio/Templar_March_20 14.mp3

[660] www.metatronminutes.net/BBS_Radio/Templar2_April_20 14.mp3

[661] www.templarinfernobookreview.com/templars_knights_tem plar.htm

[662] en.chartressecrets.org/templars/red_cross.htm

The History of the Knights Templar (Charles G. Addison) [663] [664]

The Knights Templar Talk I (Andrew Linnell) [665]

The Knights Templar Talk II (Andrew Linnell) [666]

The Knights Templar Talk III (Andrew Linnell) [667]

The Knights Templar Talk IV (Andrew Linnell) [668]

The Knights Templar Talk V (Andrew Linnell) [669]

---

[663]

www.phoenixmasonry.org/history_of_the_knights_templar/table_of_contents.htm

[664] sacred-texts.com/sro/hkt/index.htm

[665] thechristianmysteries.com/wp-content/uploads/2015/03/Talk-1.pdf

[666] thechristianmysteries.com/wp-content/uploads/2015/03/Talk-2.pdf

[667] thechristianmysteries.com/wp-content/uploads/2015/03/Talk-3-v3.pdf

[668] thechristianmysteries.com/wp-content/uploads/2015/03/Talk-4-v4.pdf

[669] thechristianmysteries.com/wp-content/uploads/2015/03/Talk-5.pdf

The Knights Templar Talk VI (Andrew Linnell) [670]

The Knights Templar and their Fate [671]

The Knights Templar, Rosslyn and Scotland [672]

The Knights Templar's Prayer [673]

<u>The Secret History of the Knights Templar in America</u> [674]

The Templar Code [675]

Tracking the Mysteries from Egypt to the Founding of America (Andrew Linnell) [676]

---

[670] hechristianmysteries.com/wp-content/uploads/2015/03/Talk-6.pdf
[671] www.languedocmysteries.info/templars.htm
[672] www.masonicnetwork.org/blog/history/the-knights-templar-rosslyn-and-scotland/
[673] knightstemplarvault.com/knights-templars-prayer/
[674] www.beliefnet.com/Entertainment/Movies/The-Da-Vinci-Code/The-Secret-History-Of-The-Knights-Templar-In-America.aspx
[675] https://topdocumentaryfilms.com/templar-code/
[676] thechristianmysteries.com/tracking-ancient-mysteries-egypt-founding-america/

THE MOTHER OF ALL FAMILY TREES

Bible Bibliographies [677]

Introduction and Other Stuff [678]

Generations 1 to 4 (Tiamat, Anunnaki) [679]

Generation 5 (Enki and Nin-khursag, Anunnaki) [680]

Generations 6 to 7 (Adam's family) [681]

Generations 8 to 12 (The Royal Line of Cain) [682]

Generations 13 to 26 (Descendants of Tubal-cain) [683]

Generations 21 to 41 (Tohwaits' (Nfry-ta-Tjenen's) Tree) [684]

---

[677] biblebibliographies.net/yahvah.html
[678] www.halexandria.org/dward911.htm
[679] www.halexandria.org/dward912.htm
[680] www.halexandria.org/dward913.htm
[681] www.halexandria.org/dward914.htm
[682] www.halexandria.org/dward915.htm
[683] www.halexandria.org/dward916.htm
[684] www.halexandria.org/dward917.htm

Generations 8 to 15 (The Royal Line of Seth) [685]

Generations 16 to 24 (Descendants of Noah) [686]

Generations 25 to 50 (Terah's Tree) [687]

Generations 41 to 47 (Generations of Ahmose, the 18th Dynasty of Ancient Egypt) [688]

Generations 48 to 51 (Moses and Miriam) [689]

Generations 51 to 60 (Generations of Kiya-tasherit) [690]

Generations 61 to 67 (Generations of King David) [691]

Generations 68 to 80 (Jezebel to Zorobabbel) [692]

---

[685] www.halexandria.org/dward918.htm
[686] www.halexandria.org/dward919.htm
[687] www.halexandria.org/dward920.htm
[688] www.halexandria.org/dward921.htm
[689] www.halexandria.org/dward922.htm
[690] www.halexandria.org/dward923.htm
[691] www.halexandria.org/dward924.htm
[692] www.halexandria.org/dward925.htm

Generations 81 to 99 (Exodus II, the Sequel) [693]

Generations 1 to 100 (The Genealogy of Jesus) [694]

Mythical History [695]

Generations 64 to 85 (Dardanus) [696]

Generations 86 to 91 (Romulus (and Remus) [697]

Generation 92 to 97 (Gaius Julius Caesar (I - IV) [698]

Generation 98 (Claudius) [699]

Generations 98 to 103 (From Rome to Camulod) [700]

Generations 100 to 111 (The Desposyni) [701]

---

[693] www.halexandria.org/dward926.htm
[694] www.halexandria.org/dward927.htm
[695] www.halexandria.org/dward963.htm
[696] www.halexandria.org/dward928.htm
[697] www.halexandria.org/dward929.htm
[698] www.halexandria.org/dward930.htm
[699] www.halexandria.org/dward931.htm
[700] www.halexandria.org/dward932.htm
[701] www.halexandria.org/dward933.htm

Generations 112 to 117 (Meroving Right Along) [702]

Generations 118 to 124 (Charlie Martel and the Dagoberts) [703]

Generations 125 to 135 (Charlie Magne and the Vanilla Factory) [704]

Generations 136 to 162 (Bolling for Ancestors) [705]

Generations 163 to 167 (End of the Line for Now) [706]

TRUTH

Ayn Rand [707]

Enigma Channel (Chris Everard) [708]

---

[702] www.halexandria.org/dward934.htm
[703] www.halexandria.org/dward935.htm
[704] www.halexandria.org/dward936.htm
[705] www.halexandria.org/dward937.htm
[706] www.halexandria.org/dward938.htm
[707] https://www.amazon.com/Ayn-Rand/e/B000APYGIW/
[708] christophereverard.co.uk

Genesology: Truth and Wisdom [709]

Michael Tsarion [710]

Want to Know [711]

We The Skythians (David Ritchie) [712]

We Seek to Serve [713]

---

[709] genesology.blogspot.com
[710] www.michaeltsarion.com
[711] https://www.wanttoknow.info
[712] https://www.gnower.net
[713] www.weseektoserve.com

About the Author

Michele Doucette is webmistress of Portals of Spirit, a spirituality website whereby one will find links to categories of interest from Angels to Zen, books of spiritual resonance, videos and documentaries. In addition, she holds a Crystal Healing Practitioner diploma (Stonebridge College in the UK) and is guardian to many from the mineral kingdom.

As a Level 2 Reiki Practitioner, she sends long distance Reiki to those who make the request, claiming only to be a channeler of the Universal Energy, thereby allowing the individual(s) in question to heal themselves.

She is the author of spiritual/metaphysical works; namely, [1] The Ultimate Enlightenment For 2012: All We Need Is Ourselves, a book that was nominated for the AllBooks Review Best Inspirational Book of 2011, [2] Turn Off The TV: Turn On Your Mind, [3] Veracity At Its Best, [4] The Collective: Essays on Reality (a composition of essays in relation to the Matrix), [5] Sleepers Awaken: The Time Is Now To Consciously Create Your Own Reality, [6] Healing the Planet and Ourselves: How To Raise Your Vibration, [7] You Are Everything: Everything Is You, [8] The Awakening of Humanity: A Foremost Necessity, [9] The Cosmos of The Soul: A Spiritual Biography, [10] Getting Out Of Our Own Way: Love Is The Only Answer, [11] Living The Jedi Way, [12] Vicarius Christi: The Vicar of Christ, [13] A Metaphysics Primer: Changing From The Inside Out, [14] The Cosmos of The Soul II: Messages and [14] Living The ED Principles all of which have been published through St. Clair Publications.

In addition, she has written another volume that deals solely with crystals, aptly entitled The Wisdom of Crystals.

The author of A Travel in Time to Grand Pré, this is a visionary metaphysical novel that historically ties the descendants of Yeshua (Jesus) to modern day Nova Scotia.

As shared by a reviewer, Veracity At Its Best "constructs the context for the spiritual message" imparted in A Travel in Time to Grand Pré.

Against the backdrop of 1754 Acadie, this novel, an alchemical tale of time travel, romance and intrigue, from Henry Sinclair to the Merovingians, from the Cathari treasure at Montségur to the Knights Templar, also blends French Acadian history with current DNA testing.

Together with the words of Yeshua as spoken at the height of his ministry, <u>A Travel in Time to Grand Pré</u> has the potential to inspire others; for it is herein that we learn how individuals can find their way, their truth(s), so as to live their lives to the fullest.

Several years in the making, she was also driven to write <u>Back Home With Evangeline</u>, the sequel. It is here that Madeleine and Michel find themselves back in the twentieth century with a message that must be shared with the world. So, too, and even more importantly, must the message be lived, and experienced, by one and all.

She is also the author of <u>Time Will Tell</u>, a uniquely moving tale that begins in the present day before weaving its way backward through time to connect a glowing thread of historic discoveries.

Courtesy of past-life regression, Michaela (Dr. Mike) Callaghan, a brilliant metaphysical scientist, in the twenty-first century, discovers that she lived as a young, noble, Cathari herbalist healer, in the Languedoc area of France, during a time when political change was in the air.

The author of <u>Ad Infinitum: Unchanging and Forevermore</u>, a love story involving Ysabeau and Ghislain, twin souls who are successful in finding each other in the physical arena of the 21st century, this is a tome that delves into both incarnation (the process whereby the non-physical essence of Source is invested with physical form; a union of the physical plane (of existence) with the non-physical) as well as reincarnation (the re-cycling of this non-physical essence into different physical forms, different time periods and different roles, in order to experience all forms of materiality, to understand each thoroughly, and to learn how to manipulate, and maintain, these forms in balance and harmony); each is the sum total of past experiences, from various perspectives, over eons of existence.

When not working as a Special Education teacher, she continues to read, research and write, exploring her personal genealogies, all of which constitute her passion.

———————❖———————

In the words of the Dalai Lama … *In order to be happy, one must first possess inner contentment; and inner contentment cannot come from having all we want; rather it comes from having and appreciating all we have.*

.